The Poconos in B Flat
The Incredible Jazz Legacy of the Pocono Mountains of Pennsylvania

Debbie Burke

For Rich, the love of my life
from Liebig Avenue

This book is based on the author's personal interviews with jazz lovers, musicians and resort professionals.

ACKNOWLEDGMENTS

There are almost too many people to thank, which is a good thing to be able to say. All the people who gave their insights and their time—and allowed me to buy them coffee—were supportive and giving beyond my expectations, making this project a total joy.

Hearty thanks go out to Bill Goodwin, Jill Goodwin, Jim Daniels, Bill Lockett, the incredible Dave Frishberg (RIP), Danny Cahn, fellow Brooklynite "Sweet" Su Terry, Sto Rubeski, Bobby Avey, Donna Antonow and Tony Diecidue. Also a huge thanks to the Celebration of the Arts (COTA) community, particularly Lauren Chamberlain, who opened the door to so many jazz personalities and offered a golden opportunity to be part of behind-the-scenes life at COTA; the supportive Cheryl Joubert; and Brian and Anita Labar, tireless and cheerful volunteers who for many years have made the festival a family affair. Camp Jazz students get a shout of thanks too: Joe Boga and Anthony Lavdanski. Also thanks to those connected with the old Mt. Airy Lodge, including the extremely helpful Susan Cooper, Bob Ferri, Steve Gilmore and Paul Rostock; and other fine musicians including Phil Woods (RIP), Vinny Bianchi, Bob Keller, Lydia Liebman, Najwa Parkins, Michael Stephans and Rick Chamberlain. My sincere gratitude also to the following: Jay Rattman, my first interview, who made it all seem so easy. He has such a positive demeanor and navigates that sax so beautifully, with grace and style. Spencer Reed, who opened up with great stories and made me laugh through the process. Nancy Reed, so kind and easy to talk to. Ka-son Reeves, an extremely talented artist who has become a good friend. He has future success written all over him. Morgan Crespo, for teaching a blockhead like me how to get a fan page going on Facebook to spread the word. Patti Keegan, with her Celtic lilt that transports you to another time and place, for her dead-on design of the front and back covers. Peter Salmon, that guy in the audience with the sketch pad at all the local concerts, whose drawings never fail to capture the essence of the moment. Malcolm Waring, who spoke freely about his father's years here as a choral genius. Lena Bloch, whom I met while buying a Miles Davis songbook. She was the reason for including an international perspective. The very terrific and knowledgeable Ralph Harrison (RIP), under whose direction in the Trinity Centennial Band it was a pleasure to play. He loaned to me one-of-a-kind music memorabilia for further study. I prized playing in the TCB under him and I already miss his lively anecdotes that made the composers come alive. Fay Lehr (RIP), who took me into the nascent days of Pocono jazz. And though we never met in person, John Coates Jr., whose genuine warmth and openness from sunny California made me wish I had been around to hear him play those wee morning hours at the Deer Head Inn. Dr. Otis French, whose excellent guidance as a conductor has encouraged me to improve on the sax, and whose accessibility and friendship has been so important to me as I wrote this book. Lance Rauh, who suggested new contacts I was not previously aware of. David Liebman, who gave me as much time as I needed and was extremely helpful. Caris Visentin, who welcomed me into the classroom at Camp Jazz and laid some eye-opening musical theory on me. Father, son and grandfather David, Davey and Dave Lantz, who all offered heartening generational insights and great tales. Kent Heckman, who showed me around his impressive recording studio and provided a perspective from the other side of the sheet music. I also had quite an experience getting to know the unique gem that is the Al Cohn Memorial Jazz Collection housed at East Stroudsburg University. Bob Dorough (RIP), who welcomed me into his home and filled my heart with the love of jazz all over again.

Tim Sohn, my cheerful and sharp-eyed editor (and now a good friend), who made things go super smoothly. My amazing friend Vicky, who reaches back into my junior high years. On long walks down Flatbush Avenue to ungodly-early meetings at the borough's first Burger King to appear in the 1970s, we would work on figuring out the meaning of life. The cows have come home, Vick.

My brother David, who has always been there for me with abundant love and support. My mom, Roz (RIP), my biggest fan, for her unwavering love, enthusiasm and selfless generosity and who is very much missed. My dad, Irving (RIP), also terribly missed and always loved, whose memory constantly inspires me to listen to my Muse. My kids, Rachel and Timothy, and my husband Rich, the love of my life, who, from my first spark of inspiration, said this was a cool idea for a book.

INTRODUCTION

This book is not intended to be an encyclopedic discussion on the detailed history of jazz or a discography of those featured, but rather a series of observational narratives on the very unique and wonderful Pocono Mountains jazz scene derived from personal interviews with musicians, historians, educators and hospitality professionals.

Definitions are as plentiful as the stars and planets. In the 1950s, Aaron Copland, in his *What To Listen For In Music* (*McGraw-Hill, 1957*), described jazz as an important entity in any discussion of tone color. The jazz band has provided listeners with novel tone effects, "whether you like them or not." It puts brass and winds in charge of the melody (typically in the form of a solo), where the background is handled by piano, bass, percussion and banjo; harmony is offered by non-soloing winds and brass. "The real fun begins when the melody is counterpointed by one or more subsidiary ones, making for an intricacy of melodic and rhythmic elements that only the closest listening can unravel," said Copland. Yet as intriguing and wondrous as jazz is, he noticed the public's ambivalent reception: "Most people seem to resent the unconventional in music . . . they use music as a couch; they want to be pillowed on it, relaxed and consoled from the stress of daily music."

According to *The Encyclopedia of Jazz* (Da Capo Press, 1984), even musicians' definitions of jazz fluctuate frequently. Jazz has "made its way out from the backwoods and dark corners of the American scene to a position of international recognition as this country's one true native contribution to the arts."

"Jazz can consume and assimilate other music," says Pocono-based drummer Bill Goodwin. "It has become more of a world music than ever . . . you can hear African, Brazilian, and Indian strains. I think it's great."

Where is jazz?

In the mountains of northeast Pennsylvania, jazz for sure is in the clubs and concert halls; also in high schools, hotel lounges and casinos; and open mics at coffee houses and churches. It's in practice rooms, art gallery openings and wine tastings. Jazz is also nurtured as a living, breathing thing at East Stroudsburg University (ESU) which houses the Al Cohn Memorial Jazz Collection. Its story began in 1988, when Ralph Hughes, a well-loved trumpet player in the Poconos who was a friend of sax master Al Cohn, approached Al's widow Flo with the idea of creating a lasting memorial. Dedicated to Al, the collection would be located at the university's library. It was conceived to have not only Al's recordings but also sheet music, books, records, reels, tapes and CDs of different eras and genres, including recordings from local jazz figures like Urbie Green (RIP), John Coates Jr. (RIP)and Phil Woods (RIP). Soon, other musicians who knew Al began to donate their materials, and the assemblage has been growing ever since. The collection has over 12,000 record albums, about 2,000 CDs, shelves packed with books and vintage jazz publications (with a vast collection of *Downbeat* through the years), photos, artwork, posters, flyers, ephemera, oral history tapes and lots of memorabilia from the Celebration of the Arts festival.

Hitting the airwaves on university radio station WESS- FM has been the perfect method for bringing this gem of a collection to the public, with jazz shows and interviews. The university also plays host to a yearly concert called "Library Alive." Here, charts that had been sleeping in file cabinets are dusted off and given their time to shine. Each year, talented local high school musicians join masters on stage to perform the selections that most of us have never heard. As an added treat, the university used to produce *The Note*, a glossy magazine with interviews, first-person perspectives and news on the jazz world, particularly as it related to the Pocono Mountains region. Until recently, it was mailed to nearly 2,000 households in 44 states and over 25 countries.

First Words on the Jazz Scene in the Poconos

The Pocono Mountains region has experienced previously unimaginable growing pains. New commercial areas emerged in the 1990s and continued appearing past the Millennium, interspersed with residential, unsidewalked neighborhoods in the woods. Often, dead ends and cul-de-sacs are backed up by state or federal game lands (meaning you cannot build there; in many cases, you cannot hunt or fish there). Commuters—reduced somewhat in rank by a crummy economy—often arise before the crack of dawn, getting on that oft-choked ribbon of a highway called Interstate 80. Many drive their own cars, continuing somehow to pay through the nose to fill up their gas tanks. Others take an express bus into New York City, spending up to four hours a day shoulder-to-shoulder with their commuting brethren. Those who notice headlights dancing on the bedroom wall at 4 a.m. are witnessing proof of yet another early-day commuter, setting out on his or her way to stay financially viable.

Around the year 2000, there was a huge spike in population throughout Monroe County. The schools were bursting at the seams and plans were percolating with the construction of new school buildings and campuses. Many so-called transplants (from Brooklyn, the Bronx, Queens, Long Island, parts of New Jersey and many other mostly eastern locales) have been here for decades and are honorary locals. Their concerns are no longer those of an on-the-move populace. They live here, put their kids in school here and are actively invested in the quality of life and how things are run.

Two things to note about the jazz scene in the Poconos that absolutely set the area apart and put it on a musical pedestal. First, it is home for two National endowment for the Arts (NEA) Jazz Masters (Phil Woods and David Liebman) and the incredible Bob Dorough of *Schoolhouse Rock!* fame. The second is a unique apprenticeship system that warmly welcomes and gently draws the younger generation into the jazz community. "Sweet" Su Terry (alto saxophonist) explains. "Older musicians feel that the essence of jazz is being lost because the traditional ways of learning are becoming so attenuated. There is an intentional community that has been set up in jazz. When they say it takes a village to raise a child, to me that's the meaning of the expression. With the collective energy of these great musicians, we are able to guide a young person into maturity through acquiring a very high level of skill." In the Poconos, not only do the masters mentor the budding talent through the Celebration of the Arts (COTA) programs and it. yearly jazz festival, it is also academia that plays a strong role in developing the up-and-comers. East Stroudsburg University (even

14

besides its music programs and community bands) had, until around 2014, offered a wide swath of opportunities through jazz programs and workshops. And maybe the best-kept secret (still) is a jazz collection that rivals any found in a university setting, the Al Cohn Memorial Jazz Collection.

The birth of jazz in the Poconos can be attributed to the hospitality industry. "If not for the resorts pulling musicians here, it might have taken much longer for the music scene to develop," said Ralph Harrison, trumpet player and long-time conductor of the local Trinity Centennial Band. The grand dames of the Poconos offered music, but largely to those upper-crust Philadelphians and New Yorkers who could afford a vacation in the country; places like Skytop, Buck Hill and Pocono Manor, which at the time hosted opera singers and concert violinists for its clientele. "Some stayed for an entire month or the summer. They weren't day trippers," added Ralph. "They wanted to know who was the artist for the summer." Later on, hotels brought in orchestras for people to interact with; vacationers now wanted music to dance by. "After World War II, things exploded. People had cars again. They had money to go on vacation. The former defense plants started making cars and refrigerators. The resorts became more modernized, booked bigger dance bands, and finally, big bands."

If pressed to come up with a singular reason that jazz was able to grow in the Pocono Mountains, one might point to a gentleman by the name of Bob Lehr. Bob had the fortune to inherit a resort called the Central House (later re-named the Deer Head Inn), *the* meeting place for jazz jammers and pros throughout the region. "The Central House became known as a jazz Mecca," continued Ralph. "It's responsible for getting jazz into the Poconos." After the resorts like Mt. Airy Lodge would end their evening entertainment, musicians would hotfoot it over to the Deer Head. "I remember John Dengler, one of the last wooden frame renters, on the third floor at the Deer Head," recalled Ralph. "John was drinking from a beer stein and lecturing about Dixieland jazz while throwing chicken livers to his cat. John said, 'Nobody sleeps when I'm lecturing about jazz.'"

In fact, Bob Lehr's wife, Fay, said it all started with Dengler. "Johnny played every instrument. He was a local Mt. Pocono boy, then a student at Princeton. He was playing at what was then the

Penn Stroud Hotel.* It was Good Friday, and the hotel said they couldn't have jazz on that day, so Johnny came to Bob and asked if he would like to have some jazz on Good Friday, and Bob said sure. We played jazz every night since."

Jazz will continue to ring throughout the Poconos as long as there are masters, mentors and students young and old who cherish it.

Matt Vashlishan, saxophonist and East Stroudsburg University band director (until COVID had other plans) has been helming the Al Cohn Memorial Jazz Library at ESU for nearly a decade and says great things are on the horizon. "Much of what I do in this collection involves getting music out there to be heard. I do this through the Water Gap Jazz Orchestra's monthly residency at the Deer Head Inn. We perform music held in the collection written by Phil Woods, Al Cohn, Dick Cohn, Gerry Mulligan, Johnny Mandel, Tiny Kahn, and the list goes on and on. I get calls constantly for donations. I can't give details yet, but we will be adding a very important big band library to add to what I feel is one of the most impressive and expansive libraries for that music. All of this news will be in *The Note*, which is still published twice a year."

DONNA ANTONOW
The Sacred with the Jazz

Her first inclination was to be a fashion designer, but Donna Antonow chose music instead, which was a natural for her—piano and vocals, to be precise. "I played before I knew what I was playing. It came easy," she says. "My first gig, I was 15 and played with other kids. We did a few local gigs. At 17, I performed solo in a restaurant, then in college I got more gigs." Although trained in classical music, her first performances were pop tunes like those of James Taylor.

Hearing Thad Jones was the clincher for a career in jazz. He was the music director at William Paterson University, where Donna received her bachelor's degree in music and then a teaching degree for K-12. "I hated classroom teaching with a passion, but I had to make money. I did it for ten years, couldn't wait for the day that I would quit."

There's music in her family: her father's side is all professional musicians. Her maternal uncle played upright bass, and her grandfather and uncles played horns, sax, clarinet and trumpet.

She lived in the Poconos for over 20 years and hails from northern New Jersey, where most of her gigs started out, where she has returned. "Even in New York, there's a minimum to go into a club, but it wasn't like that years ago. Used to be I would go have coffee and dessert, sit and hear music all night. At the Deer Head, you can still do that. You just hang and listen to the music." The highlight of her career so far has been playing piano for jazz vocalist Mark Murphy. Among her favorites are Bill Evans, Keith Jarrett and Sonny Rollins, and she loves the Great American Songbook titles. Her main gripe when performing is that most young people do not know the standards, and they ask her to play Led Zeppelin. "I used to say 'forget it' but at least it's good for the tip jar. You just get done crying your heart out doing 'The Thrill is Gone' and somebody asks 'can you do Billy Joel?' Oy!"

She recorded two CDs, one with Dave Brubeck's former bassist and another with Bob Dorough. She now teaches music in New Jersey and started a new direction, playing the pipe organ in a Parsippany, New Jersey church where she also sings. "I like it. I prayed and got this gig. You never know what you're going to end up doing, and the next thing you know you're doing it."

BOBBY AVEY
A Cat Reflects

The work involved in developing one's style is not for the faint of heart. Pianist and former COTA Cat Bobby Avey says many piano instruction methods involve primarily an exercise in memory. But that's not as meaningful a perspective as looking from the inside out. "Most children are taught piano lessons and they learn the outer shell of a piece, the correct notes and rhythms with the correct dynamics," he observes. "It's great to have a sense of accomplishment, but if you liken that to memorizing a speech in a different language without ever having checked out the context, you never know what you are talking about." By high school, Bobby was immersed in music. "I knew how deeply I was pulled to this, but I can't say that I understood the scope of what it meant to dedicate your life to it." He joined the COTA Cats (a band that serves as "a gateway to the jazz community") and studied with some outstanding musicians. "Dave Liebman has been a musical father to me. He travels all over the world, yet he's always had time for me."

Other influences include jazz pianist Wynton Kelly (with the Miles Davis Quintet), Herbie Hancock, McCoy Tyner (a pianist with the John Coltrane Quartet) and French composer and organist Olivier Messiaen.

A former resident of the Poconos who now makes Brooklyn his home, Bobby continues developing his strong musical ties here with his work with David Liebman, who plays on several tracks of his 2010 CD, *A New Face*. Bobby won the 2011 Thelonious Monk Competition for composition, and he was awarded the 2011 Chamber Music America New Jazz Works/ Commissioning and Ensemble Development grant. In 2013, he released his first solo piano album and played in the David Liebman group Expansions.

DANNY CAHN
Gabriel Blows His Horn

Danny Cahn made the trumpet his life's work. From the time he was a fifth grader in the Stroudsburg school system, he persevered and found himself playing in *Jesus Christ Superstar* on Broadway. Danny reminisces on his good fortune in having the school band conductor at the time, Ralph Harrison, as his very first teacher. "I remember him making it all so interesting," he says. Danny comes from solid musical stock. His uncle, Jack Cahn, was a New York City school teacher who, post-retirement, became the musical director at several Catskills resorts. Classically trained, Jack also played with swing band leader Les Elgart.

"I was lucky to get into the Manhattan School of Music," Danny recalls. "When I got there, they took me under their wing and I let them sweep me away." Though the level of talent he witnessed was admittedly "scary" he was not intimidated but inspired. In 1971, after graduation, he went on the road with a 32-piece orchestra and the cast of *Superstar*. Also on the tour bus was fledgling mega-star Andrew Lloyd Webber. It was a fantastic job he says. He met his wife, Marsha, of 40 years there. She was a viola player. They toured together with the Mahavishnu Orchestra with John McLaughlin, with Barbra Streisand and with Johnny Mathis. After a year with *Superstar* he got off the road, remaining in New York. The market there offered abundant work for freelancers, particularly in advertising (writing and performing jingles) and with big bands.

After those flush years, the synthesizer came on the scene. "It kind of replaced the larger orchestra, and work started to dwindle down for studio players." Broadway orchestras were recruiting more freelance players and it was a scramble trying to get the best jobs. No regrets: he's had a lot of great leaders. For one, Maynard Ferguson. "I was 25. Maynard was the greatest trumpet player ever played with." He also counts in Doc Severinsen and many other established studio trumpet players. In 1980, he played on the funk band Parliament's ninth album, *Trombipulation*.

"When it was time to take my pension, I came back to the Poconos. Now I can play for my own benefit." In 2011, he finished a Westbury, New York job playing with Johnny Mathis. He performed with David Liebman's band, at the Scranton Jazz Festival, at Delaware Water Gap's COTA and he gives private lessons. "Basically, I just wait for the phone to ring. I play every day and keep my chops up."

RICK CHAMBERLAIN
Brass Master and COTA Co-Founder

"I love music of all types and try not to put it into boxes." So said the man whose sophisticated résumé demonstrated a facility with multiple genres. Rick Chamberlain was principal trombonist with the New York City Ballet Orchestra. He played with the Westchester (NY) Philharmonic, the American Composers Orchestra, the Brooklyn Philharmonic and the New York Pops; and at venues like Carnegie Hall and the Brooklyn Academy of Music. He toured with Gerry Mulligan's band, Chuck Mangione and drummer/band leader and NEA Jazz Master Louie Bellson. That's the short list.

Rick played trombone since he was five because his dad played it. "It's probably the most in-tune instrument there is. It's got one moving part so it's the simplest one." When studying music in school he learned piano, flute and clarinet.

A top-notch band program at his Bucks County, Pennsylvania high school led him to Phil Woods' jazz camp in 1965. He played in small ensembles in school and had the good fortune to play in the Greater Trenton symphony orchestra at age 16. "I started studying with [session musician and jazz trombonist] Wayne Andre in New York in tenth grade. He took me around to see what he was doing, and I got to do things like filling in for him in Clark Terry's Big Band."

What a turn of luck awaited him as a young trombone player. At age 18, when Rick graduated from high school, Wayne, who had a house in Delaware Water Gap, asked him to come up, spend the summer and take care of his place. "He was going back and forth from New York. I was holding down the fort here and driving his little MG—it was a real opportunity!" It was then that he was introduced to the jazz scene at places like the Deer Head Inn, and he found work at the former Mt. Airy Lodge, Tamiment Resort and other local hot spots.

There has been much evidence of Rick's entrepreneurial

spirit. He was the enthusiastic co-founder of the successful and growing Celebration of the Arts festival held every September in Delaware Water Gap. Besides his gigging, he continued to be heavily involved in the planning and prep work for COTA. He helped with the music schedules and the PR, garnering a fair amount of local and regional coverage ("The big three are WNTI, WRTI and WVIA. It's hard to get into the New York press.") COTA also received play on radio personality Jim Wilke's show *Jazz After Hours* on National Public Radio. Along with the curator of East Stroudsburg University's Al Cohn Memorial Jazz Collection, Rick came up with the idea of "Library Alive," a unique way, on an annual basis, to showcase previously unheard (or under-heard) jazz charts. The concert brought young local talent—high school musicians—together with jazz veterans, sometimes importing them from New York or the West Coast. In 2011, for example, sax man Lou Marini joined student musicians on stage. "That year they put together a program commemorating the jazz loft scene and Zoot Sims. We're not going to rehearse," said Rick. "It'll be just a jam session. Everybody loves to play Al Cohn's music. We'd just have a whole bunch of music available to play."

Perhaps, Rick theorized, the jazz pilgrimage from New York City started well before the '50s and '60s lounge musicians who sped over to the Deer Head Inn after hours. Maybe it was Golden Age's Fred Waring, whose choral orchestra in the 1930s and onward spent time in Shawnee-on-Delaware (where Fred lived and rehearsed his musicians). Today, the era of live big bands at resorts may be a sweet memory, but jazz finds its way around, somehow. Witness COTA, the healthy Camp Jazz, the enthusiastic students throughout the Poconos who choose a musical career path and the two NEA Jazz Masters who continue to mentor and inspire. "There's an energy here that affects all the artists, painters and photographers. Delaware Water Gap itself is a unique structure with very high spirituality. I believe in the forces of Mother Earth, and it comes together here." Rick passed away in 2015.

JOHN COATES JR.
Historic Influence on the Pocono Jazz Scene

The story of how jazz grew in the Poconos hinges upon the fortunate turn of events that placed a young "Johnny" Coates Jr. on the piano bench at the Deer Head Inn.

He came from Trenton, New Jersey and became a proficient pianist on the New York/New Jersey circuit. At 13, he was the youngest musician to join the musician's union in Trenton. In 1955, he ventured west and performed at the Deer Head Inn, "the only jazz place around" in the Poconos. He got turned onto it by a Trenton jazz trombone player by the name of Bob Jenny and immediately fell in love with its owners, Bob and Fay Lehr. "I would tell people in other areas where I would play about this wonderful place in Delaware Water Gap, and little by little other players would come to the Poconos looking for gigs there," he said. In 1957, Coates went on the road with tenor saxophonist and band leader Charlie Ventura, playing big-name clubs like Birdland and The Blue Note. "It was really fun and dreamlike." What an accomplishment to play the major clubs in the city . . . but at the same time, he said, "these places weren't as interesting as the Deer Head. There is a freedom at the Deer Head, and I liked that setting." He described other places as more commercial and restricting, where there was a tacit obligation to play many of the same songs every evening. At the Deer Head, there was more space to express yourself musically.

When 1962 rolled around, he was asked to be the Deer Head's house pianist. To some, that's the sweet kernel of the Pocono jazz scene, when it became its own entity and gained steam. "By then, I was a fairly experienced jazz player," he said. According to many accounts, musicians would fly over after their resort gigs and grab a seat to hear Johnny tickle the ivories and maybe sit in with him. He'd play from 10 p.m. to 2 a.m. which later stretched to three in the morning.

In 2010, Johnny suffered a stroke that mostly affected his left hand. Through time, his functioning had been greatly restored. At the time of his passing in 2017, he lived in California with his music, his partner Lisa, and a great view. "I can look out one window and see the ocean. On the other side I can see the mountains."

His best times were where he made his strongest impact. "My days at the Deer Head were more meaningful to me than anything. I got to play some famous places, but those years were the best. I look forward to returning there."

Cool and Pithy

"I was a piano major at William Paterson, minored in voice. Thad Jones was the music director at Paterson, and when I heard that, I said 'this is it! I have to teach myself this!'"
—Donna Antonow

"The Grammys just dropped Latin Jazz from its list. The only thing we invented is baseball, Mickey Mouse and jazz. That's unconscionable. There will be blood in the streets."
[Latin jazz was reinstated in 2012.]
—Phil Woods

"I heard a Bill Chase single, 'Get It on,' that had all these screaming high trumpets. That's the hunk of music that got me started on jazz."
—Jim Daniels

"Scales, arpeggios and sight reading are the most important skills a musician can develop. Without them you cannot do anything."
—Lance Rauh

"When I was about 13, I determined that *The Man With The Golden Arm* had a wonderful jazz score. When I heard Shelly Manne playing [on the soundtrack], I decided I would be a jazz drummer for real."
—Bill Goodwin

"As a composer or songwriter, sometimes you have a visit from the Muse, but you can't wait for that. You can have this faint longing to write a love song for a certain situation and you're not sure how to do it, it's festering there."
—Bob Dorough

"One year at COTA, four guys played on one piano in a 'piano extravaganza.' It was nice to see that camaraderie among guys who are competitors for work. I've always been impressed by that."
—Dave Lantz III

"I was in the service, stationed in Germany, and played first trumpet with 16th Army Band, the 389th Army Band in Ft. Monmouth, then the Army band in Virginia. It kind of shored up the big holes in my musical education."
—David Lantz Jr.

"It took me a long time to get comfortable with scatting. I had to learn to trust myself. It's not planned, and it has to be off-the-cuff. My repertoire has gotten bigger as I go forward."
—Nancy Reed

"I remember the very beginning of COTA as a scattering of people on the hill. When I see all the people enjoying themselves, the sound technicians, the stage and the lights, and how everything has grown, it's a really great feeling."
—Cheryl Joubert

"The goal of transcribing is not to regurgitate the solo. It's not a chunk of ice where ideas are frozen together, one after another."
—Caris Visentin

"The more the audience appreciates jazz, the more open it is to its styles and colors. I believe the audience is carried away to the world of free imagination, spontaneous and brilliant decisions and individuality emerging."
—Lena Bloch

"Don't go into music looking for a career in music, go looking for a life in music."
—Lydia Liebman

"My mother's a conductor. I would hate being dragged to concerts. Something just clicked in me when I was older."
—Joe Boga

"There's a big history in Delaware Water Gap of jazz musicians and there are probably a couple of reasons for that. One of the main reasons is that the New York City's union laws stated if you had any kind of record where you got busted for even low-level narcotics like marijuana, you had your union cabaret card taken away and you could not work in New York City. That led to a certain exodus from the city to the Poconos. They had to make a

living."
—Steve Gilmore

"Jazz originally was dance music in the swing era. Then it became artsy. I'd like to see it come back to where you listen and dance to it. My greatest thrill in my band La Cuchina was when people danced to us."
—Vinny Bianchi

"Always sit down with the intention that you're going to get better than before you sat down."
—Davey Lantz

"Mt. Airy Lodge led the way. The entertainment absolutely put us on the map."
—Susan Cooper

"Bars and restaurants today are just not paying. We'd be working more if we accepted less."
—Tony Diecidue

"Bob Newman and Bob Dorough were the two musical spirits of the Poconos. Bob Newman imported a lot of musicians from New York and Philly. And if Bob Dorough was around, people flocked to him like a jazz guru."
—Dave Frishberg

"My third-grade music teacher was an awful, vicious person, the first person I knew who brought her problems to work. But she taught me something that feeds my family."
—Spencer Reed

"I value spontaneity over anything else. If I feel myself about to play something I've played before, I'll deliberately change course. Since you are surprising yourself, it will engage the other musicians and inspire different contributions."
—Jay Rattman

"The musicians that were playing in show bands were dying to hear jazz when their gigs were over, so they would come to the Deer Head. It was very magnetic, and I was really fortunate to be the main guy there."

—John Coates Jr.

"Jazz musicians are hooked by listening, that's the best way to learn. I could teach you scales, arpeggios and lines, but the only way to learn is you've got to develop your ears."
—Bob Keller

"I was very interested in medicine, and I really wanted to be a surgeon. Since I had polio as a child, I had a lot of interaction with doctors. I could see my mother's face when one of my leg doctors would say something to her about what was next. It was like God speaking—very impressive to a young cat. Music took me to another path. When I saw Coltrane, it was so powerful, I had to find out about it. The rest is history."
—David Liebman

"The biggest challenge in conducting: thoroughly knowing the score you want to conduct. You've got to know what to expect when you drop the baton."
—Ralph Harrison

"I always knew I wanted to live here. The landscape really appealed to me, and the fact that there was this awesome jazz community here and what seemed to be a very advanced mentoring system where new generations of musicians were coming up."
—"Sweet" Su Terry

"I had no idea what jazz was about. I was not a jazz fan. Now, I think it's great because, along with the tremendous skill involved, there is a wonderful looseness and the improvisation element makes it exciting."
—Kent Heckman

"Some soloists just play without relating to the music. I don't think that is the spirit of jazz. Make your solos match the chords. Improv is building on these ideas and connecting it to the music."
—Dr. Otis French

"Do people go out to hear jazz music? They stay home. Jazz has never been exposed to the mainstream media. If jazz had been played more on the radio or popular TV shows then younger

people could develop an interest. It's confined to public radio, college radio stations and satellite radio."
—Paul Rostock

"Actually *being here* really brought the words 'jazz' and 'community' closer together in a very tangible way. The jazz folk that populate this area, and that includes listeners as well as players, constitute a very special bunch of people. My wife Kathleen and I were warmly welcomed into the fold and that acceptance has been a part of our lives ever since."
—Michael Stephans

"When I first heard Nancy [Reed] sing, I felt a connection. Hearing her natural voice sounded like what I thought my voice could be like. I wanted to learn from her."
—Najwa Parkins

COTA:
The Celebration of the Arts Festival

A three-year-old girl in pigtails sporting a green and pink striped shirt and pink leggings bounces and bops with her own improv dance moves. She's grooving to a young and surprisingly sophisticated musician known as Grace Kelly, who wails away on the sax along with ultimate sax master Phil Woods. The little girl is in the designated dancing-only section that crosses in front of the open-air stage at the Celebration of the Arts, where lucky music lovers get full-frontal jazz for two-plus days. Attendees are treated to an astoundingly talented lineup that would be described as impressive to any jazz aficionado on the planet. The year? 2010.

Once a year, for a smidge more than a weekend near Labor Day, jazz comes to the Poconos in a demonstrably splashy way. COTA—the Celebration of the Arts—is Delaware Water Gap's musical pinnacle, and over the years has drawn thousands from its kickoff on a Friday night (replete with local original art) to its wrap-up just past suppertime on Sunday. They come from local towns, from New York, Philly, Jersey, across the nation and around the world from places like Australia, Japan and Germany.

In 2022, the event celebrated its 44th year. It continues to evolve, offering more musical diversity to the delight of current and future jazz lovers (scores of families bring their little ones in hopes of cultivating a lifelong appreciation). The collectible COTA posters and strung-up display of event t-shirts illustrate the longevity of the festival and the breadth of talent which has played under the skies and stars with the Pocono Mountains as a backdrop. Posters start appearing in late spring, placed by volunteers in strategic spots including the growing college town of neighboring Stroudsburg (a short interborough bridge away from East Stroudsburg University), a variety of the state's visitor centers and as far away as Sarasota Springs—even up to Canada. "We cover probably a 100-mile radius really well," says Lauren Chamberlain, daughter of co-founder Rick

Chamberlain.

Planning begins well before any PR efforts are under way. A dedicated cadre of volunteers form the COTA committee that seems to grow every year. After a brief post-event respite, the committee and board begin the deconstruction process, recapping and critiquing, and then start to map out the next year's celebration. Volunteers work tirelessly; sometimes whole families, from kids to parents to grandparents, are involved: manning security, selling tickets, handing out programs, working as the stage crew, cleaning tables and helping the vendors who all must have some local affiliation (restaurants, artisans, non-profits like the Boy scouts and religious organizations). One long-time volunteer, Cheryl Joubert, ran the booth that sells the musicians CDs. She moved to the Poconos from New Jersey, brought here by her dad Ed Joubert (one of the co- founders of COTA and owner of The Bottom of the Fox Bar and Restaurant that featured homegrown jazz and rock). Adds Cheryl, "I started coming here on weekends as soon as I got my driver's license. I thought the town was so cool, filled with artists and musicians."

The festival is well developed by now. There is no more scrambling for talent; it's fully branded, attracting repeat bands as well as newcomers. Musicians are abundant and available, all hoping to participate in the yearly jazz offering. "We have a lot more people than we can use," says drummer Bill Goodwin. So musicians are rotated from year to year. Some of the original performers from COTA's early years are grandfathered in and play every year. Returning musicians can expect to be combined in new ways with different personnel. The pairing of Grace Kelly—a young sax musician with very keen scatting abilities—together with Phil Woods is a good example of how the beginner and the established equal beautiful music. The variety of acts is a testament to the planners' understanding that its growing audience has wide ranging tastes.

COTA became a 501(c) non-profit organization under the umbrella of the modestly sized Delaware Water Gap Chamber of Commerce. Soon it was clear that COTA was becoming too big to remain a division of the chamber, resulting in it incorporation and status as a 501(c)(3). Rich Chamberlain, COTA co-founder and a trombonist who played for the NYC Ballet

Orchestra, looked back at the genesis of the event. "Phil [Woods] and I keep saying to each other 'look what you started!'" Rick remembered their colleague Ed Joubert and said, "Every year we write a letter to Joubert saying this is another mess you got us into. He was the problem solver. He built the gazebo for the church."

The genesis of this long-running event was explained by Phil Woods, who said it started because the musicians in Delaware Water Gap were constantly having jam sessions, and maybe something bigger could be made out of it. "I was there with Ed [Joubert] and Rick [Chamberlain], and we said, we should move it outdoors, put it on a couple of risers. The rest is history." It became a tool to raise money for building a sewage treatment plant in the Gap since the town had a "wildcat sewage system that ran straight into the [Delaware] River," according to Rick Chamberlain.

He continued: "One pipe started by Phil's house, went down the street under the sidewalk and into the middle of the river. So it was a legitimate concern. We started the festival and raised money for it." However, it was an expensive event to run, and not much was raised at first. "But over the years we sank thousands and thousands into the borough. It helped with parks and recreation, the fire company and the Dutot Museum, all that stuff." Construction of the sewage system, a 10-year process, was finally completed in the late 1980s. For Rick, his activism evolved into civic service. "I got elected to the borough council of Delaware Water Gap and for four years served as president of the council."

Paul Rostock is an established bass player who started playing professionally at the age of 15 and got into the Pocono resort scene beginning at age 18. He's had a long career touring with Frank Sinatra Jr.'s band, gives private lessons and is a faculty member at Moravian College in Bethlehem, Pennsylvania. He's performed at COTA regularly and says of the experience, "More young players are coming into their own. COTA is still one of my favorite festivals. It's a kind of reunion. That was the whole premise, for all the musicians living here to get a chance to play for the community."

Year after year, COTA's featured musicians participate for the sheer love of being part of an enchanted weekend. We know this because of the democracy of the experience: the honorarium is a flat rate. Musicians' fees for playing are the same whether they play once, twice or more during the festival, whether novice or international master. "We don't make much money, but it's pure," noted Woods, referencing the fact that COTA has never had a corporate sponsor. So much more would be possible with a sponsor, but Woods said it was the only way to keep it sacred. "We could get Coca Cola in a minute, but they'd mess with it." Rick Chamberlain agreed: "There's just so much pressure to turn it into a sponsor-driven event, which we can never do. This was started by musicians, for musicians, as much as for the audience." It is a struggle, though. There are layers of costs that make things like grants (which are getting harder to secure) even more crucial; costs like the professional sound systems, portable toilets, garbage management. "We used to get a lot of grants from the state, but they pulled back because we were doing a good job of it," Rick lamented. "It's a shame the powers that be don't want to realize the arts drive culture, which defines a society."

Not only won't the event sell out for a corporate underwriter, but COTA planners won't bring in a big name just for the sake of bumping up attendance revenues. "What people don't realize is there's a local connection with everybody who plays on that stage," said Rick. Start bringing in the household names in jazz, and they won't play for what amounts to a stipend. But it's really better this way. "Everybody's there because they want to be there. It's an opportunity to be part of a community."

JIM DANIELS
Brass Dreams, Jazz Reality

At age five, Jim Daniels was old enough to hold a ukulele; in kindergarten he graduated to bluegrass style banjo and piano. "In fifth grade they offer you the choice. I wanted to play oboe. I liked the sound of it. My father said no. Then I said okay, French horn, but my father said why don't you try trombone, which was my third choice." That stuck.

Early in his career Jim had been recording jingles and subbing for a lot of Broadway shows (*Annie, Sweeney Todd*, and *Carousel*). He made a habit of playing the Village Vanguard, The Bottom Line, the Blue Note. It was also a period of commuting to the Poconos from New York for gigs with fellow trombonist Rick Chamberlain. "He invited me out for a weekend to play in a band when he was living in Delaware Water Gap. I came to visit and hang out. I ended up staying a day or two extra every time." The trips worked on him, and in 1981, what with the country living and trees all around, Jim decided to move here.

The first Celebration of the Arts festival he attended was in 1980. Smitten, he became COTA stage manager for many years starting in '81. "I was playing as a guest artist at first. That got me in the door." In those days he also performed at the Tamiment Resort and Conference Center, Mt. Airy Lodge and Unity House in Bushkill, which hosted a Dixieland picnic every weekend. All three are no longer standing, but at the time they represented steady work. However, after relocating, he experienced a decline of freelance work coming from the city. "If they don't see your face, they forget about you very quickly. So my work slowly got less and less. They have short memories."

He secured a position at East Stroudsburg University in 2004, imparting knowledge of jazz and pop, teaching piano class and serving as director of the jazz ensemble. What was the magic of the Pennsylvania Mountains? "I got this feeling that if you had some census data you'd find, per capita, a higher percentage of musicians here than anywhere in the world."

Jim, who also plays tuba, headed down about an hour away to the Lehigh Valley, doing shows like *Crazy for You* and *The Sound of Music* at Muhlenberg College and DeSales University. He subbed in New York City occasionally (*Wicked*, and at the New York City Ballet with Rick Chamberlain). Other musical endeavors included the Jazz Artists Repertory orchestra (JARO) program at East Stroudsburg University and a local Dixieland outfit called The Dixie Gents. He's composed and arranged for brass ensembles, chorus and jazz ensembles.

COTA CAMP JAZZ
Delaware Water Gap: Training Grounds

Camp Jazz, a one-week program hosted by COTA for student musicians in the Poconos, serves students from age 12 and up. One recent class was comprised of 36 eager young adults who strolled into the Deer Head Inn and the nearby Church on the Mountain in Delaware Water Gap, toting their horns, drum kits, guitars and vocal cords. They enlisted to learn and to have a blast. Both were delivered. The model was half peer-to-peer interaction, half instruction and encouragement by professionals who are, in many cases, quite renowned musicians.

Among other special classes, some very eye-opening ear training was provided by oboe and English horn musician and composer Caris Visentin. She is the wife of NEA Jazz Master David Liebman (saxophonist). The premise of effective ear training is to form an acoustic and muscular memory of how a note feels. For example, Caris asked students to sing their lowest comfortable, clear note. Do this every day for about a year, she told them. Each time, check it against a keyboard (or other instrument) to find out what note you are singing on an average basis. "The lowest note then becomes the reference note and can be used for finding the key center," she informed. She also spoke of visualization improvisation: the ability to visualize the space between the notes and then vocally setting for each note.

Soloing needs to be internalized to the extent that it becomes "a part of you, and it is very easy to embellish it and make it your own. When you're singing, if you miss a note, you just come right in. You have trained your ears to go ahead." If it is just a physical exercise you do with your fingers on your instrument, the minute you break that dance, you can't go on. This is because it is a physical memory, not an internal melodic memory. The goal of improv, she says, is not to copy what others have done, but to internalize the improvised solos of master musicians in order to lay the foundation. She also cautioned students not to fill every silence with sound. "It's incredible how nervous you get when there's space in a solo. You need the space for the notes to have their effect. The space is setting up your next entrance."

Caris—who studied with Boston-based jazz pianist Harvey Diamond and with New York's Lee Konitz (composer and alto saxophonist associated with the Cool Jazz movement)— spoke of a "sketch book" that becomes one's personal improv portfolio. Pull out those ideas that really killed you and use them as a catalyst. They are ideas for future use. "In the end, you'll just pick things like a collage. What you really like, what you could use, what's just okay." Most of all, she emphasized to her students a strong connection between instrumental skills and vocalization. Do not, she advised, go to your instrument until you sing the notes, using your own scat language to re-create the sound. Then, when you play it, it's going to "go down like water . . . those ideas begin to have life once you extract them
and make them your own."

Between the classroom instruction, break-out sessions and some downtime to jam and become acquainted with other students, instructors and professional musicians, the week at Camp Jazz is a fast one but represents a unique experience the participants will always recall. Apparently, the formula works; one needs only to track the students' progress from Monday to Friday (and note the current success of the graduates) to see how effective the program is.

So, just what are some of the Camp Jazz grads doing now?

Joe Boga (trumpet): Now a member of the legendary group Vince Giordano and the Nighthawks.

Najwa Parkins (vocals): She attended Temple University for jazz studies and is now a Philadelphia-based singer, songwriter arranger and bandleader.

Lydia Liebman (vocals): She attended Emerson College and Berklee College of Music and ran a jazz show on the radio. Today she runs Lydia Liebman Promotions and has been named a "Forbe 30 Under 30" in music.

Anthony Lavdanski (bass guitar): He attended the University of Toronto to study music. With his roots still firmly in jazz, he has turned to barbering and is the owner of Truman Barber Co. in Boulder, CO.

Jay Rattman (saxophone): He received his master's from the Manhattan School of Music and moved from the Poconos to New York City, performing at Jazz at Lincoln Center and appearing on *The Late Show* and *The Tonight Show*. He plays other genres as well, including klezmer, classical chamber music and free improv.

Then, as the class members asked for advice, this is what some of the panelists had to say:

Joe: My mom bought me a Louis Armstrong CD as a birthday gift and I never opened it up. I let it sit for six months. Then I was really embarrassed so I said, I will at least put it on once. I heard "Potato Head Blues" and something sort of snapped in me. I really connected. Listen to a wide variety of really good music and to people who play music very well, and your career will develop.

Najwa: There was always music playing in my house since I was born, not necessarily just jazz. Then I started trombone with the band. I had a great teacher who introduced me to a lot of great people in the jazz community in Delaware Water Gap. I started singing and I guess music has been a constant in my life. When things get hard, I say what else can I do? I don't want to do anything else. You need to start building confidence but not being cocky.

Lydia: I was exposed to music at a very young age. My dad played John Coltrane's "Crescent" when I was born. I used to go to Birdland and I hated it; I would sit on a sax case and sleep. I learned piano at age seven and I hated practicing. One day, I was going through my dad's CDs and found *The Classic Quartet—The Complete Impulse! Compilation*. When I heard "Acknowledgement" from *A Love Supreme*, something changed. Suddenly I felt attached to the music. It became clear I couldn't be involved in anything else.

Anthony: I was 11 and I noticed everybody was happy in the jazz club no matter what happened at work. I always thought it was cool how you could play music and make everybody happy. As cliché as it sounds, follow your heart, play what you want to play and make music you want to love. Don't get caught up in feeling you're not good enough. If you just stick with it, everything will work out.

Davey Lantz (piano): From a young age, I always knew that I was living in this great area. I can't imagine doing anything else. I started on the violin. It was terrible, I'm still in agony. I did that for 10 years and asked my parents if I could quit every year. I didn't even like piano very much. I fell in love with music when I picked up a guitar, which was the first thing I wasn't forced to do. It's really important not to do it because of external pressures or because someone says 'you have to listen to this record.' stay focused, take a break, and come back and be mindful of what you are practicing. I've had to undo a lot of bad habits from when I was younger. Practicing is work but it should be rewarding to you, and you will enjoy the result.

ANTHONY DIECIDUE
Smooth Knocks on the Door

The Pocono-based smooth Jazz band got a foothold at Mt. Airy Casino Resort with a regular gig and started building a fan base. But about a year later, they lost the booking. To get new work, the band needed a video, says drummer Anthony Diecidue, so they found a studio run by Tony Bennett's son. "It was a big mistake," says Anthony. "The audio was great, but the video was terrible." That was the official demise of smooth.

Anthony reinvented himself musically as the Tony D Jazz Trio, with a new sax player (their original woodwind player had moved to Arizona) and a pianist. The group played gigs in local clubs and bars. Anthony also played in a blues and classic rock band with a guitarist from outside the Poconos. "I like smooth jazz much better, but the bar and restaurant owners want to stick with the safety of what they know, like a guitarist who can sing rock'n'roll."

The drummer's challenge, he notes, is keeping polyrhythmic: being able to do two or three things simultaneously with different parts of the body. He has a good ear and can learn a song after hearing it once or twice. But smooth as a sub-genre of jazz is not for everybody, and many do not think of it as even being related to jazz. None of this matters to Anthony.

"I pick musicians because there is something about smooth jazz that grabs them. But it's a real tough sell here in the Poconos. I hope I can keep it going and increase the size of my trio, at least to add a bass player." There is a nearby market where Anthony says smooth jazz is very hot. "The Berks Jazz Fest in Reading [Pennsylvania]. Of all the places on the planet, Reading is a destination for smooth jazz."

Anthony started out by taking drum lessons at age 10, piano lessons at age 11, and he dabbled on guitar. He learned by listening to the radio, not by reading music. In school, he played snare drum and cymbals in marching band. And now, by day, he's an optometrist. "When I was a senior in high school, I knew that I would go into the health care profession. I toyed with the idea of becoming a pharmacist or a chiropractor, but in my first year of college, when I met some friends who were going into optometry school, I decided that was what I wanted to do."

Two drummers in particular inspired him. One is Dave Weckl, who has played with Paul Simon, Madonna and Chick Corea. "He was voted one of the 25 best drummers of all time, and once you hear him play, you'll understand why." The other musician is Mike Stephans, a musician, author and educator who lives in the Poconos. "Not only a wonderful human being and good friend," says Anthony, "but one of the most talented drummers I've ever had the privilege of knowing. He's a guy who can play any style of music on the planet and do it like he's been playing it his whole life. His love of music is contagious, and he truly makes the drums a musical instrument and not just a time-keeping tool."

There are a number of out-of-work musicians in the Poconos, and Anthony laments the general lack of venues where the community can enjoy all the genres of music that now exist— smooth included. "My jazz friends say that smooth jazz is really just pop with some jazz flavor, but whatever it is, it reaches me and a lot of other folks too. I think the Poconos is ready for this genre of music. Smooth jazz is generally found in urban areas like New York and Philadelphia, but we have a lot of urbanites living in the Poconos these days and they're looking for more diversity in their musical entertainment."

David Liebman (photo credit Matt Vashlishan)

Nancy Reed (photo credit Chris Drukker)

Spencer Reed (photo credit Bud Nealy)

"Sweet" Su Terry (photo credit Dan Demetriad)

Bill Goodwin (photo credit Laurie Samet)

Trinity Centennial Band (art by Peter Salmon)

Jay Rattman (photo credit Jonno Rattman)

Tony Diecidue (photo credit Mike Brygider)

Lena Bloch (photo credit Mildred Klaus)

Vinny Bianchi (photo credit Danielle Jordan)

BOB DOROUGH
The Devil May Care . . .
But Not Bob

In 2011, the 34th annual COTA festival celebrated the contributions of musical titan Bob Dorough. Actor Peter Coyote was on site, discussing his family's ties to the festival (his father owned a farm near Delaware Water Gap that drew many jazz musicians to the area). In his introduction of the esteemed Mr. Dorough, Peter said, "Here's a guy who graduates high school and stays an extra year so he can play in the band." When the applause died down, he added, "Bob is the most superlative and talented musician that I ever knew." Just how did he get that way?

Born in Arkansas in 1923, Bob Dorough's early years were marked by family moves throughout the state. Bob's first love was the clarinet. "I played in the high school band and told my parents I was going to be a musician. They didn't fight it a bit." The family ended up in West Texas, a location Bob's father decided upon in order to join his brother, a farmer. By then, Bob had forgotten about music. "I was doing farm work for my uncle, and I thought I was going to be a cowboy." In 1937, the school bandmaster, a displaced Chicagoan, drafted Bob into the band after he earned impressive test scores in pitch and timbre recognition. "I had tried out for football, but I was as thin as a rail. Suddenly I was in the band, playing in the last clarinet seat, and thinking wow, I'm going to be a musician!" The director gave Bob clarinet lessons and harmony lessons, and Bob tried to write music for his band. But the director had a prejudice against jazz. "So one of the drummers said to me 'let's start a jazz band.' We got stock orchestrations on the q.t. from DownBeat. We were trying to play 'In the Mood,' and in the meantime, I was picking stuff out on the piano." Bob's first college experience at Texas Tech was interrupted by being drafted into the Army in 1943. His military career included the special services band, where he learned more about performing, arranging, composing and singing. In 1946, he resumed his education, completing his bachelor's degree in composition in three years at the prestigious University of North

Texas.

Upon graduation, he headed immediately for New York City, where he remained for about a decade. His GI Bill ran out while at Columbia University in 1952, so he became a professional musician. Soon he grew enamored of The Great American Songbook, operetta and Tin Pan Alley, as well as Bird and Dizzy. "Of course bebop became my main goal and inspiration, but I did a little singing in my own apartment," he said. In 1957, he went to Los Angeles to make a recording. Although it didn't work out, he ended up staying on the west coast for about three years playing bebop and singing, then headed east again to the city.

"The minute I got back to New York, I called one of my best jazz friends, Bob Newman. I had jammed with him. He was a great tenor man. I said hey, Bob, I'm back. He said, are you working?" Newman had been appointed to lead the band at Mt. Airy Lodge in the Poconos and offered Bob the piano chair. Newman explained the place like this: "You know, it's sort of like the Catskills but not so Jewish."

It was 1960. "I was skeptical, but Newman wheedled me until I said yes. I had an apartment on a tentative basis. Things were kind of slow in the summer, but it was so much fun I stayed for the winter and another summer, then resigned." Almost two years later Mt. Airy was busy again, thriving to such an extent as to sustain two bands. "I was the leader of the second band. We played shows and dance music." On Saturdays, after playing the last dance, they'd hurry over to the Deer Head Inn to hear John Coates Jr. and catch his last two tunes of the night. Things were still slow on the performing end, so Bob started to write jingles just to make money, working with bassist Ben Tucker. "I learned how to handle the clock," he recalled. "Jingles have to be 30 or 60 seconds, sometimes 20 seconds or even shorter." These were flush times, allowing Bob to buy his home in the Poconos where he has been ever since. Bob also worked for Chad Mitchell (of The Chad Mitchell Trio) and co-produced *Spanky and Our Gang.*

"Writing jingles led me to this set of people who gave me the idea to put the multiplication tables to music," said Bob. It came about in 1971 after David B. McCall, president of the ad agency McCaffrey & McCall, reached out to Bob for help with his young son who was having trouble with math in school. "He said, 'my boy can't memorize the times tables but he sings along with Jimi Hendrix and he gets all the words. Why don't we put it to music and call it *Multiplication Rock*?'" McCall had contacted other jingle composers at the time, but, said Bob, "They all came up with a really simplistic approach, thinking that children are little idiots. When he told me what he wanted, I was highly inspired. I had a chill up my spine." The first tune Bob submitted was "Three is a Magic Number" and when McCall heard it, he "flipped out" and immediately put Bob to work. Other assignments, collectively dubbed *Multiplication Rock*, followed quickly.

It took him two years to write and record 11 multiplication songs, all tested at the Bank Street School of Education, a teachers' college in New York City. "McCall wanted to produce a phonograph record of the songs and sell it to affluent parents and schools and libraries. None of us were thinking of TV at all, but the art director, Tom Yohe, began drawing a storyboard of 'Three is a Magic Number' and it became *Schoolhouse Rock!* in 1973 on ABC TV." Other subjects were introduced, and Bob became very busy on *Schoolhouse*. Keeping on task was simple, added Bob: "Johann Sebastian Bach produced so much because of his deadlines. Every Sunday he had to have a new cantata. You get a specific commission and very little time to do it. If you don't do it, you don't get the gig."

Multiplication Rock was a fully developed unit. Bob was working as an arranger, singer, songwriter and record producer to create the *Schoolhouse* segments. Each song had to be precisely three minutes. He sang eight of the 11 songs himself. "I was able to employ some of my jazz friends like Blossom Dearie from the cabaret world. She sang 'Figure 8.' Grady Tate [jazz drummer and singer] did 'I Got Six' and 'Naughty Number Nine.' I had studied the new math at Columbia and showed them the tunes. I took it all the way up to 12 and I even delivered a song about zero. That flabbergasted them completely." Even though the series was arranged and played with a jazz sensibility, rock was king at the time. "We couldn't call it *Multiplication Jazz*. You'd be crazy. They'd say that's for old men." *Schoolhouse Rock!* lasted 13 years on the Saturday morning cartoons on ABC. After multiplication, they switched to grammar, and Bob was no longer the exclusive songwriter, although he did write some of the grammar songs.

In the '70s, Bob's performance career took off. He traveled all around the States and to Europe. His first trip to Oslo was in 1987. The manager of the Oslo Jaz Hus heard Bob singing on a Miles Davis LP and said, "I've never heard anyone like that." So he found Bob by telephone and brought him to Oslo, where he played the club three times. This developed into the Oslo Jazz Festival. In 2011 Bob returned from his sixth trip there, performing in the 25th annual festival.

Come 1995, he signed with the prestigious jazz label Blue Note Records and recorded three CDs for them (*Right on My Way Home*, *Too Much Coffee Man* and *Who's On First*). In 2002, his trio was chosen to represent the U.S. Department of State and The Kennedy Center as an Ambassador of Jazz and Blues. They toured for a month, playing over 20 workshops and concerts, in 13 cities, in six countries.

A brilliant documentary on Bob's incredible life called *Devil May Care* was produced by Beth Bogart and Steve Berger and previewed at the 2011 Celebration of the Arts. It included clips of vintage Dorough and featured his remarkable insights into a life of music. The film (named for Bob's inaugural album of the same name) did not appear to find enough funding to get off the ground and into the hands of executives at public television; it is still listed as "in production."

Bob passed away in 2018 at the age of 94. He said he wanted to keep working as long as he could "get to the gig" and added, " love to sing and play for people who want to listen to me. remember my first year of college. I would stay up all night copying music so I could hear it. It's my curse, but I love it."

DR. OTIS C. FRENCH
Jazz Thoughts from a Civil War Buff

A band leader has to be a skilled technician on the baton, a superlative listener and an individual who can inspire his or her musicians, imparting a deep appreciation of music to others. Dr. Otis French enjoys a full life in music, not only by conducting and directing but sharing his love through education. The former director of bands at East Stroudsburg University, he began a lifelong relationship with music when he started trumpet in the fifth grade in Kentucky. In junior high, he switched to baritone (euphonium) because the school band didn't have any euphonium players. In high school, he played trumpet in concert band and jazz band. "When I graduated high school and went into the Army, euphonium became my instrument," he says. Not wanting to leave any brass stone unturned, he then learned trombone and tuba, followed by keyboards and composition. He's also literate in woodwinds and wants to learn the strings.

The notion to create music from the tip of a baton came when he was 21 and in the Army band in Fort Dix, New Jersey. "We had a new band commander, Alfred Tapia. He was a euphonium soloist who became a conductor. Probably the best leader I ever had. He had a passion, a gift and knowledge. It always stuck with me that he transformed the ability and image of the Army band in a short amount of time. We were a professional military band doing difficult literature. It got around how he shaped it and transformed it." Three years later, Otis got the opportunity to learn military conducting, which he says was the real start of his career.

An avid Civil War historian, Otis melded his passions for music and military history with a decision to write a doctoral dissertation at the University of Maryland on using Civil War-era brass band music to compose modern arrangements. This was a way to teach Civil War music history to high school and college bands, and audiences. "I found a Civil War reenactment band in

Brodhead, Wisconsin, and spent a weekend with them. They had a complete set of old sax horns—the only place where a complete set of soprano through bass saxhorns can be found—and I videotaped them being played. They did demos of all the instruments." One extinct and rarely seen instrument he included is the ophicleide, which resembles a sax, but the keys work in the opposite way (rather than depressing the keys to form a note, the music is emitted by opening the keys). With a requirement to include original research in his paper, Otis wrote arrangements for two Union and two Confederate pieces, and produced a DVD demonstrating how the valves work with the different instruments. "There were instruments that you play over the shoulder that threw the sound backwards, and cylindrical instruments that wrap around the body. I showed a period band playing music as they sat with their backs to the audience." He tracked down sheet music that was published by the Moravian Music Society in North Carolina. For the Union Army pieces, there are no complete sets of music existing. To join it all together, he found a band training manual that was used by the Union Army. "Union pieces are a lot more martial [relating to marches], up-tempo and patriotic. Confederate pieces are more musical. They're folk ballads. Even their marches seem to be a little smoother."

Otis speaks of jazz being the purest American art form. "You find jazz in everything. Rock music is based on jazz chords, and the solos in rock music came from it. I like the freedom in jazz and hearing how different professional players come up with their solos." Yet he admits that he doesn't have a particular gift for improvisation. "With Dixieland, I play with the melody. I'll take the tune and mold and shape it, but I haven't done the legwork to do improv." Is there room for improv in a college band situation? "If we have those who want to solo, they can. We are fortunate we had quite a few who were willing to try."

Some of his favorite composers are Beethoven "because of the depth of thought he put into music," Sousa, because of his stature in the band world and for putting bands on the map, and contemporary composer Mark Camphouse, whom Otis knows personally. "I analyzed a lot of his pieces and wrote articles on them." He has trained himself in score realization: looking at a piece and knowing how it is going to sound. "I like the challenge of that. I try first to get it in my ear before

22

hearing somebody else's interpretation."

In the university setting, he directs several community bands in the Midwest as he is no longer with East Stroudsburg University (which made severe cuts in its music program). When the bands were active, the traditional flow was for community members (some professional musicians, some hobbyists) acted as mentors and role models for the students; however, sometimes students reciprocated by sharing their gifts to help a community member.

The jazz scene developed in the Poconos, believes Otis, because of the proximity to New York (a location he calls "a hotbed for jazz") without the high costs associated with city living. "This has become a little satellite for professional players, to our benefit. I see not only jazz but also all the arts can thrive here and should thrive here."

DAVE FRISHBERG
A Fondness for Swiftwater

Almost 60 years ago, New York-based piano great Dave Frishberg looked to the west and decided to call Swiftwater, Pennsylvania, his new home. He and his wife rented a cottage there for $75 a month. In return, he got to be a stone's throw away from the burgeoning jazz situation in Delaware Water Gap.

"We sublet our [Greenwich] Village apartment and became country people. I needed to get out of New York," said Dave. "I had a couple of gigs with Jerry and Dottie Dodgion at Mt. Airy [Lodge]. They had a quartet, and I played a few weekends." (Jerry played sax and flute, and his wife was a drummer.) At Mt. Airy, Dave worked in Bob Newman's band and then took on weekend performances at Tamiment Resort, in 1968, where his wife Stella sang. By that time, he felt, jazz started to die down as a national phenomenon, and pop music and rock'n'roll were taking prominence. The resort demographic wanted commercial tunes, though, not jazz. How Maestro Newman got around this was ingenious: although his band would play what people wanted to dance to, he cleverly morphed them by giving them jazzy arrangements.

The annual Celebration of the Arts festival was an amazing experience for Dave and impressed him with the spirit of community. He spoke particularly fondly of one of the Poconos favorite sons, Bob Dorough, with whom he worked on the *Schoolhouse Rock!* music. He called Bob "one of my special heroes of life, and a lot of people feel that way." All told, Dave's Pennsylvania years were rewarding. "I was playing new music every day. I became a better sight reader."

Dave moved around a bit more—stopping for 15 years in Los Angeles—and had relocated to Portland, Oregon, until his passing in 2021.

FUTURE OF JAZZ
Where To, What Now?

Kent Heckman built Red Rock Recording studio next door to his farmhouse in the Pocono countryside in 1988. At first, the guy who grew up playing rock 'n' roll guitar had no jazz clients. But once he added a Yamaha piano in 1989, the jazz came around. "With such a strong jazz scene here, it was exciting when they found me. They were used to going to New York and New Jersey, and at first, I was intimidated because I didn't know too much about jazz. After a while, I realized the trick was just to capture their playing as clean and pure as I could, and they really appreciated this. Plus, they are a great bunch of people." His development as a recording scientist came about by necessity. "When I was first putting together the studio, the guy who was supposed to do the wiring for me never showed up, so I learned to do it myself. As my studio grew, so did my technical skills." He gets a lot of referrals and repeat business and observes the changes over the years in the industry. Studios in New York have been closing like crazy, he says, because of their sky-high rents and the upward trend of musicians who have their own home studios, thanks to digital advances.

To some, gender bias still plagues the jazz scene, says "Sweet" Su Terry. "A big problem today is that in spite of all the great women players out there, the music industry is not booking women the way they book men. They are not promoting women the way they show interest in male musicians. It's unbelievable." Others lament a general shrinkage in the market for all musicians. Former Fernwood Resort house band leader Sto Rubeski (Sto and Company) says that in the late 1970s, bands were populated by a good number of musicians. Performing at the local resorts, his band had four guys and a female vocalist. "We played six nights a week. As years went on the bands went from five to four pieces, and from six to four days a week. Through the '80s people played less and less. Now these resorts have a Saturday night band, but that's it." The hotels have all reduced live music to practically nothing. "We had a good thing there for a while. When they started cutting down, it was all over."

Steve Gilmore, bass player, agrees. "In the '60s, '70s and '80s, I was just about as active as I wanted to be. Those jobs are not happening. All of a sudden, the economy thing hit and the bottom kind of fell out." Too, while technology has advanced the industry in unthinkable and wonderful ways, "it knocked the hell out of the music business. Live music is not that important now." Musicians have been replaced by machines: "what used to be one guy strumming guitar ends up being karaoke now." Steve toured with Phil Woods, gigged at Birdland and Dizzy's, played the COTA Festival and traveled to places like Japan where he performed after the devastating 2011 tsunami.

Why did the work dry up at the resorts? Jim Daniels responds: "A lot of resorts just closed. Mt. Airy hires show bands from New York and New Jersey. There is not a lot of Pocono-based talent there. Most of the work now is in Bethlehem, Allentown and maybe Scranton." Yet the prognosis for the local scene is positive "I think jazz is healthy here, because of COTA and its sequel COTA Camp Jazz," he adds. "There's a talented young group of musicians who became unbelievable musicians because they studied with people like Dave Liebman and Phil Woods. Work is getting harder to find, and it's harder to put a tour together. But the artists are the only the ones who can help change the planet."

Michael Stephans is an established and multi-talented jazz drummer, award-winning published poet and a Ph.D. in Education who has taught at the University of Miami, Pasadena City College and Bloomsburg University (Pennsylvania). Although he was not residing in the Poconos during the jazz heydays of the 1950s and 1960s, he can relate to the demise of steady work. "The very same thing happened years ago in Vegas when a lot of the hotel orchestras were replaced by canned music, and the club date bands were nixed in favor of DJs playing ear-splitting music at weddings and bar mitzvahs. However, having spent many years out in L.A. as a full-time musician, you do what you can to survive. And it's certainly not easy. I have a deep and abiding respect for those who are tenacious and who do what is necessary to persevere."

An optimistic perspective on the future of jazz comes from vocalist and bass player Nancy Reed. "I think it's going to get better

Younger people are digging jazz more, and people always want to go out, so it might as well be jazz."

BILL GOODWIN
Heart Beats Like a Drum

As a wee kid, Bill Goodwin felt he had a natural rhythmic sensibility. "I played the pots and pans and sang before I spoke." His formal entrée into music came with piano lessons at age five ("it's compulsory in my family, just like reading the newspaper.") Yet he fell in love with the sound of the sax, particularly as handled by Lester Young. "My parents had a large collection of jazz records and knew some musicians, so it seemed natural that I would be exposed to it." Dad was a successful film actor and radio personality, and mom was a dancing Goldwyn Girl who was also in the chorus with Lucille Ball in Busby Berkeley's *Roman Scandals*. He described his parents as Adlai Stevenson Democrats who encouraged all family members to participate in the lively dinnertime discussions of politics and current events. "We could all talk at the same time. There was yelling but not in an angry way. It's sort of like being in a jazz group. When balanced properly you can all 'talk' at the same time and it's a great conversation."

His junior high in North Hollywood had a decent band program and so Bill signed up. "I got a sax, and my parents got me a better teacher than I deserved." While the sound in his head was influenced by Lester, Al Cohn and Zoot Sims, he couldn't replicate it and in fact admits his sound was terrible. Then fate intervened.

"My best friend had a snare drum I used to borrow. I beat on it and played along with records." Bill became a good reader of the percussion parts, and finally in the last semester of eighth grade after pointing out to the band director that there were 15 saxes, he was asked to play in the drum section. When the family relocated to Palm Springs, he started high school as the biggest guy in school at 6' 5". He made the official switch to drums, playing baritone and bass drum in the marching band. "My career as a drummer was off to the races." At the tender age of 13, Bill played the local youth center, and later, "we did boogie-woogie and rhythm and blues, and we were cautioned not to do the 'dirty boogie.' We'd drink Manischewitz in the back of the car. We were exposed to marijuana to great benefit, or so it seemed at the time." He was feeling great about his playing (never having taken lessons) and thought that enthusiasm and readiness was all it took. "I hadn't developed very much in terms of technique." His dad passed away when he was 16 and the family moved back to Los Angeles. Bill started meeting musicians his own age. "When I was 17, I could play with really good musicians, and I sounded good. But between 18 and 19, I fell apart. I just didn't have the sustaining technique. You have to practice your scales, get the proper grip and go through the rudiments."

Then as a parking lot attendant for NBC Studios in Hollywood, he had a practice pad, a pair of drumsticks and a radio. He practiced in between telling people where to park and continued to play gigs. At 19, he left his day job and played music exclusively. He became inspired by (and befriended) drummer Shelly Manne (featured in 1955's *Man With The Golden Arm*); Stan Levey (who backed up The Monkees) and drummer Mel Lewis (The Thad Jones/Mel Lewis Jazz Orchestra), "guys like my Jewish uncles, who would cajole me and help me get better." His education went smoothly due to an excellent ability to both listen and memorize. As a kid and a rabid baseball fan, he memorized the entire encyclopedia of baseball cover to cover. "I'm sort of like that with the jazz scene, with its history and tall tales and apocrypha. I still love it."

COTA CATS
Groomed into Jazz

In 1981, a seminal letter went out to high school band directors in the Poconos, which turned out to be a pivotal juncture in bringing up the next generation of talent. In that year, the esteemed NEA Jazz Master Phil Woods (a resident of Delaware Water Gap) sent a letter to every high school band director in the county (Monroe County has four school districts, each with multiple schools). The missive was an exploration of sorts, testing the waters to see if there was any interest in an extracurricular music program that would develop jazz prodigies. "The student musicians in the area were good but not plentiful," says Lance Rauh, former band director of Delaware Valley High School in Milford, Pennsylvania (in neighboring Pike County). The sole response came from a local band director who was a trumpet and flugelhorn musician, who brought the pitch to his students and was favored with a good response. That year, young musicians called "COTA Cats" (for the Celebration of the Arts event) met and practiced, gave local performances and then demonstrated their chops at COTA, the annual Delaware Water Gap jazz festival. Every year since then (excluding the lockdown), the growing COTA Cats program produces more skilled musicians who delight the community and outward beyond the Poconos' geographic borders.

"I joined the jazz band in high school, but I never practiced," admits Lance, a trumpet player who is a former COTA Cat (vintage 1995). When he received an invitation to join the Cats he initially stressed over it; that is, until he got serious and buckled down. When a scheduling conflict arose between jazz rehearsals and the high school baseball team, he realized the COTA Cats represented a unique opportunity. With the gentle persuasion of his new teacher Nelson Hill (who enthused, "You've got to do this!"), Lance made the commitment. "I got a letter that said to show up at East Stroudsburg University. I remember my uncle driving me down. I was nervous as all heck. I wasn't really very good at the time," he recalls. The organization was still in its infancy, tackling only four tunes (the bands program at ESU is now defunct). Lance went on to become a high school music teacher and band director in the nearby Delaware Valley school district. His career also took him for a few years to Susquehanna University in Selinsgrove, Pennsylvania as a lecturing music teacher. He returned to the COTA Cats and became involved as an alumnus, feeling it was his duty to pay it forward. With an insider's perspective, Lance worked on his doctoral dissertation about the Celebration of the Arts. "I think COTA is a pretty neat model. I cannot seem to find anything like it in my research. There is a choir in Norfolk, Virginia, but it's not for education, it's really just performing," he observes. He describes the experience as a "continuous reciprocal community" where the younger generation is polished and welcomed warmly into the jazz community. Upon completion, the students are poised to help bring up the next set of artists. "When you come through the system, you become a mentor and professional somewhere else in the world."

In 2001, a letter was again sent out soliciting regional high school band directors, to infuse new local talent into the COTA Cats. This time, three responses came in: Lance ("How could I not give back?"); a music teacher from nearby Hazleton; and the newly hired band director in East Stroudsburg.

"Well over 1,000 kids have been through the program," noted Phil Woods. "It doesn't matter whether they become pros or not. It's a very select group. I get emails from kids who say they never forgot that summer." Many students have parents who were COTA Cats, and that was very rewarding to Phil. "I sleep a little better knowing that the kids know who Charlie Parker and John Coltrane were."

RALPH HARRISON
Comfortable on Both Sides of the Podium

Ralph Harrison had bowed out of one of his loves, conducting Trinity Centennial Band, in the early 2000s, but that didn't mean he wouldn't be forever associated with it in the minds of music lovers throughout the Poconos.

The concert band continues to be a growing group of local musicians from their teens to their 80s, formed over 30 years ago by Russell Speicher, a much-beloved music teacher from the Pocono Mountain School District. Billing itself as "A Community Band For The Poconos," it is a summertime phenomenon, folding up just as the school year starts. It was originally formed as a celebratory ensemble, lauding the 100th anniversary of Trinity Episcopal Church in Mt. Pocono.

A modest guy, Ralph had been well known for his sharp and skillful direction of the band. But wasn't just his manner of wielding the baton that energized his students. During rehearsals he would delight band members with descriptive stories that brought to life the known and obscure composers like Sousa, Offenbach and Franz von Suppé. Until his passing in 2022, he played in other small bands that circulated around Monroe County, including an "oompah" group assembled by the local German American Society called the Jolly Rhinelanders and Riverside Rhythm.

Sometimes, a solitary and fleeting event is all it takes to light the spark of inspiration. Ralph got his start on the trumpet when he was 10. "I saw Harry James perform live in his white tux jacket with his golden trumpet, and that was it. I wanted to do that," he recalled. Ralph borrowed his father's trumpet (his dad did not play professionally), taking private lessons until the age of 16. "From 18 to 20, I was bumming around the country as a freelance trumpet player. I played everywhere and everything I could. played square dances and traveled with a polka band. I played lots of concert-in-the-park venues and even a short stint with the show *Holiday on Ice*." When he was 20, the Korean War broke out. Military units were deployed, and Ralph ended up in an Army band in Germany. The band played military installations, providing functional ceremonial music and entertainment for the troops, and special assignments for visiting generals, with an occasional U.S. congressman. The band also served as a public relations unit, introducing Germans to the American music experience. While traveling through southern Germany, his band was assigned two railroad cars, one for personnel and one for instruments and equipment. The band also played on a weekly radio program on Armed Forces Radio Network which was accessible to the German civilian population. At the base, band members were able to take college classes taught by members who had been drafted and had their own college or teaching careers interrupted by military obligations. "Upon discharge, I was well prepared for my own college experience," he said.

Ralph graduated from Wilkes College (now Wilkes University) with a bachelor's degree in music education. Then, with a coveted Dean's Scholarship Award for the highest possible GPA, he moved on to get his master's degree in conducting from Trenton State College (now The College of New Jersey).

His teaching career began in the Stroud Union School District (today's Stroudsburg Area School District) in 1956 at a yearly salary of $3,200. His assignment was to establish a district-wide elementary instrumental program that would serve as a feeder program for the upper grades. He remained with the district for 38 years, teaching all levels including concert and marching bands in high school.

In the mid-1980s, East Stroudsburg University opened its band program to members of the community. Now, musicians who were teaching had an opportunity to become active players again. Ralph participated for many years, playing the brass line-up of trumpet, trombone, euphonium and tuba; he also stepped in as a substitute conductor.

Ralph's musical roots spanned from across the globe. His grandfather, John Camel Harrison, emigrated from Scotland to work the mines as did many of his countrymen. John played baritone in the early 1900s with other Scots near Wilkes-Barre, Pennsylvania. The band was appropriately named The Thistle Band of Plains, Pennsylvania. Inspired by this, Ralph's father began playing trumpet, and when Ralph was 10, his dad handed it down.

When Ralph was a senior in high school in 1947, his father told him, "I think you need a better trumpet." But things took an unexpected musical turn: when they answered a classified ad to trade up for a better horn, it seemed another instrument presented itself. "By the time we got there, the guy swapped it for a bass fiddle," recalls Ralph. "My dad said 'okay, we'll take it,' so we stuffed it in the trunk of our Pontiac." With no bass teachers in the area at the time, Ralph became a self-taught bass player. "The new trumpet came later," he added.

When he moved to Stroudsburg in 1956, trumpet players in the Poconos were "a dime a dozen," but bass players were scarce. "I found a lot of gigs with big bands and combos as a bass player, thanks to Dad's decision to pick up a second instrument for me."

Being a resourceful self-starter, Ralph launched several bands on his own. "Just before I went into the Army, I started the Ralph Harrison Orchestra. We had four saxes, two trumpets, a trombone, a piano, a bass and drums. We played a lot of school and community dances and had to join the musicians' union. At that time, contract scale was $7 a man for a three-hour job, double for the band leader."

When the art form was called "jass," Ralph played with Tommy Cullen, a well-known member of Fred Waring's orchestra. "We played a lot of tunes, some of which I had never played before. So I had to learn quickly, expanding my own repertoire." Tommy knew how to program a set of tunes to keep dancers happy, and he played to the audience in true professional style.

Throughout all his performing experience, Ralph was also developing and refining his conducting skills. His journey as band leader includes the Dallas (Pennsylvania) Community Band, the Wilkes College Concert Band and the East Stroudsburg University Community Band. From 2002 to 2010, Ralph followed in the large conductor's footsteps made by the talented Russ Speicher who was the original leader of the Trinity Centennial

Band.

Leonard Bernstein had a lot to say in *The Joy Of Music* (*Simon and Schuster, 1959*) about the art and science of conducting, its complexities and nuances. For instance, on counting the beats with one's baton, Mr. Bernstein said a conductor "must convey the character of the music . . . there are infinite numbers of ways . . . of beating *two*, each way showing a different quality." Just to be conducted by Ralph Harrison made it obvious that he possessed a broad understanding of his craft and a full appreciation of his responsibility on the podium as described by Bernstein. Counting his personal conductor favorites as concert band institutions Sousa and Edwin Franko Goldman (a prominent band conductor from New York City at the turn of the 1900s), Ralph said, "I try to conduct in the style of them, not necessarily imitating them." The development of his own personal style evolved through experience, which in turn sharpened his skills of attentiveness and concentration. The conductor's advantage is actually being in front of the total sound. He added, "When you are sitting in a section, you are somewhat deprived of the sounds the others are making. As a conductor, you hear the blend and the contribution of each section. The bottom line is, you have to know the score."

BOB KELLER
Don't Sanitize the Music

You play Broadway, you've got to be flexible. "I'm a doubler," said Bob Keller. A slight misnomer since he plays multiple instruments: all the saxes, all the clarinets and all flutes. "It's what you have to do to play in New York."

Bob worked almost 50 years doing commercial work including in the pit orchestras on Broadway. In the 1960s he played in Buddy Rich's big band. "I always played jazz but never made a career out of it until I retired. I wanted to make a good living and build a pension so I would be able to play the music I want. That's exactly what happened." Raised in Queens, New York, his entrée to the Poconos occurred in the early 1970s when playing at Tamiment under leader Bob Boucher. Even then, he was no stranger to Pocono jazz musicians: he knew trumpet player Danny Cahn from recording dates in New York City, Phil Woods from the Manhattan School of Music where Bob taught for 15 years in the jazz department, and Rick Chamberlain from Chuck Israels' National Jazz Ensemble in the 1970s.

Having moved around a bit in New Jersey, Bob met his wife at a 45th high school reunion in 2003. "We couldn't afford to live where she was in Long Island. We had friends in the Poconos, and I knew there was a scene here. So in 2006, we moved to Milford [Pike County]." He gave flute workshops and played COTA and the Scranton Jazz Festival.

"I take jazz gigs as they come. If they come my way fine, if not that's okay." His daily regimen included practicing up to four hours a day on both sax and flute.

One regret about the state of music today was that society has moved beyond acoustic instruments. "Young people from their early ages do not hear acoustic music as much as electronic instruments. The music they are interested in has changed." In 1968, when he started on Broadway, orchestras had 30 musicians now any of the large orchestras that exist have been grandfathered in, such as *Lion King* which has 24 musicians. "Even rock 'n' roll can be played with fewer instruments. As long as electronics are involved, they don't need to have big orchestras."

Most acts now come pretty much self-contained, and the need for larger groups has gone the way of the wind, he observed. "You can go to Broadway and put on a show. The house used to require 19 musicians, but now they'll say, 'well, the music doesn't demand that.' The union used to be very powerful 50 years ago, and in the old times certain theaters like The Palace would require 26 musicians." Elton John's *Aida*, he pointed out, only required 15 musicians. "Because so much music on TV is done with the synthesizer, that's what people hear. They don't miss a big string section," Bob added. At most, a theatrical production will hire a string quartet and flesh out the sound with electronics.

There's something just as onerous as the shrinking pool of available work for live musicians: digitization, which is edging out the artist. "What's coming down the road is the 'VO,' the virtual orchestra. One man sitting at a computer keyboard, everything recorded. He can accompany the show every night with all those sounds that are electronically reproduced." The VO, also known as VPO (for Virtual Pit Orchestra), could mean the demise of a livelihood for many musicians. Despite a moratorium on the VPO for 10 years brought on by musicians' protests in Los Angeles, Seattle and New York around 2001, it's had a devastating effect on the artists. "I've seen 60 years of acoustic music change to electronic music. If you go to the pop concerts, that's what you are going to see. There's a crew in the back that controls the amplification and also the pitch." Most of the artists are not trained musicians, he added. "They put out a beautifully refined product, and you'd never know how weak they were unless you asked them to sing a tune without the use of those devices."

"Jazz musicians like Su Terry, what a marvelous musician she is. Also younger people like Jay Rattman. Davey Lantz is just an amazing musician. It's great being with the young talent. I never worked with Bob Dorough until I came here, and I've gotten to know Phil [Woods] really well. When he puts that horn in his mouth, oh man, am I glad to be here with him listening to this. He is a frighteningly good artist."

THE LANTZ FAMILY
That Good Old Generational Jazz Thing

The Lantz family exemplifies the term "generational jazz." Dave Lantz III, who plays electric bass as well as upright, taught in the East Stroudsburg School District for over 20 years and directs several local choirs. His jazz roots are evident.

After college, he worked for now-defunct music publisher Shawnee Press in Delaware Water Gap. "I learned some things about the publishing business, and meanwhile I played gigs at resorts," he says. In the 1980s he had his own variety band, and to supplement that income he did freelance work including editing, composing and arranging. Toward the end of the '80s, playing work in the Pocono resorts started to die down. "I saw the handwriting on the wall and went back to my original plan, which was teaching music in a public school." Dave III continued to play gigs, arrange and compose choral music for publication, conduct a church choir, as well as other work for a variety of music publishers.

As a little kid, his son Davey (IV) was surrounded by music. "It's there in the house all the time, and it becomes part of you whether you want it to or not." Grandfather (David Jr.) was a high school music teacher; he played gigs with Tommy Cullen, Paul Hubbell and Bob Jenny. Father and grandfather had played together locally. "My mother was a part-time private piano teacher and a very fine singer," says Dave III. "The generation before that, my mother's parents were extremely well known in Atlanta. My maternal grandmother was a concert pianist who had been known to occasionally sit in with the Harry James orchestra and my grandfather was a semi-professional singer who was featured on the Major Bowes Amateur Hour on radio that ran in the 1930s and 1940s. My grandfather had a beautiful bass voice. His feature song was 'Old Man River.'" Dave III's son, a graduate of Juilliard, shares a passion for music with his four sisters. But Davey developed his talent to a much further degree, and he

74

enjoys being in the thick of the musical arts that city life serves up. Says Dave III: "Davey is aiming high, musically. He wants to get to the top of the game. His mother and I feel good that we were able to provide him with teachers who made a difference."

Davey's mom, Marti, is a musician as well who regularly played gigs in Pocono resorts and hotels. Says the father: "The music and the work are what brought the two of us together."

There was an early cognition in Davey's mind that he was living in a special part of the world as far as jazz is concerned. It's what provided him the inspiration to do this for the rest of his life. It wasn't always that way. His musical baby steps were with the violin, but he admits playing was "agony." For 10 years, he never felt at home playing violin and told his parents he wanted to quit. He played sax in a school band; fooled around on drums and tolerated (at the time) piano lessons. "I fell in love with music when I picked up a guitar. It was the first thing I wasn't forced to do." Yet the real source of his musical ambition was piano lessons with Eric Doney (now passed), and piano became his passion. Davey's first gig was on piano at age 13 at the Deer Head Inn. His dad had picked up the upright bass again, and they formed a trio with drummer Joe Walmach. "I was excited and nervous because the Deer Head was the first place I started going to see music. It was my favorite place. I looked up to everyone there."

Following high school, Davey jumped two states and entered Juilliard, earning a BA in Jazz Performance. Immediately he was awed by the number of contacts there, by the sheer number of opportunities and venues. "I've just been practicing for years, and now it's about doing it."

Now grooving on the urban environment, Davey says that unlike the more gently paced Pocono Mountains, New York is not one big community. "In New York City, there are so many different types of musicians, all with different viewpoints. There's a lot of opportunity to play various styles, but you have to know what you want to do if you want to master anything," he observes. Even very accomplished musicians are not considered particularly special because of the mass of people who know their way around their instruments. The tight competition in the market means you have to work extraordinarily hard to reach the top, but the challenge feeds him, driving him forward. "It's like starting over. The rewards are great if you keep at it."

His grandpa, David Lantz Jr. (who passed in 2022), started it all, what with his adventures in piano and trumpet. And don't forget his upright bass from the Army. Now there was a story.

"I was in a bivouac in Germany. We were in Stuttgart for three months. We got a group together; it was Harvey Cousins on alto, and Roger Acker, my best friend, who is a natural pianist and also a teacher. They didn't have a bass player. I had purchased a bass while we were in the 16th Army Band. The tuba player wanted to play string bass but discovered he really didn't like it. So he decided he would sell it and have a tuba made in Germany while he was there. He asked, anybody want to buy it? I scraped enough money together to buy it, $85. I had one bass lesson previously and played enough to know I couldn't play it.

"We made money playing in the officer's club, did a few jobs there, then it came time to go home. And then, the scene of scenes: I guess I'll have to sell my bass, but I have no idea how. Roger said maybe we can carry that home. You've never lived if you've never been on a troop ship on the North Atlantic seas with wall-to-wall men, many throwing up around you. How would we do it? Roger said if you can carry a duffel bag and a bass, I can take the other stuff. We can try and get that home.

"Now it's time to prepare to leave, and I say, let's give it a try. Took the strings off, the bridge is down. I stole an Army mattress cover and dressed it and then I put it in that cheap flimsy cover that was no protection but it kept the scratches off. We started our journey, taking a long train ride to southern then northern Germany. We had no permanent assignment other than being in the barracks and going to bed. I'm carrying this bass around because I can't leave it anywhere." Someone suggested that he goes to see the commander, so he let Roger guard it. David located the commander, who told him to bring it over and he would then be sure it got on the ship.

David continued, "The next day I get on the ship, and I draw guard duty. Roger is out, he's looking all over the ship, but he can't find the bass. I'm saying well, whatever, I hope the SOB enjoys it. So we're going to leave in 10 minutes, since every once in a while the Army is on time. But I can't leave my post. Anyway, the ship's got these big doors to load cargo. Five minutes before the ship sails down the pier, here comes this big truck with big boxes of files of all the men who are going to be on the boat. On top of the truck waving around is my bass. I get off duty and down in the hull. There's the bass laying there with hundreds of men milling around and two guys sitting on my bass. Roger finds blue chalk and writes 'please do not sit on this, fragile.' It sat in the hull for nine days.

"Back in the States at Fort Dix, we get off the boat in a big, long line of soldiers. I'm carrying the bass and the duffel bag. Finally, we march into the train. When we got on the train in Germany, the bass had to take up a seat. Some lieutenant says *whose is that, you can't have that here, it takes up the place of a man.* But we're getting out of the Army so I'm not paying any attention. I had to carry it around and hide it. Then, as soon as I got out of the service, my dad put it in the car. I got home. I hadn't seen my mother in 18 months, hadn't seen my wife in months, or my daughter since she was born. I opened up the bass in my mother's living room expecting to see a bunch of toothpicks. There was not a mark on it, not even a crack."

Looking back, David reported a rocky start to his musical career growing up in Newton, New Jersey, with piano lessons that ended abruptly, as soon as he heard he was supposed to play in front of people at a recital. However, he used to love to visit his aunt, who lived in a farmhouse in New Jersey. On the third floor was an organ that he took to with gusto. In his first year of high school, he started trumpet. "Within two weeks, I was in the band doing a parade, but I almost quit music then and there because I couldn't play or read the music, and you are moving back and forth and walking, trying to read the music, and I said 'this is for the birds.'" Come sophomore year, his family moved to East Stroudsburg, where the high school had a well-disciplined band directed by the late Clement Wiedinmyer. David started as last chair in his sophomore year but ended up first chair in 1947, his senior year. He said, "We had a big trip to Johnstown [Pennsylvania] for a competition. We won Class C. It was a big deal for us." West Chester Teacher's College, at the time, led him to a teacher's license, and what goes around . . . he returned to a career in education in Morris County, New Jersey, where he was the supervisor of music at West Morris Central High school. He developed music programs for New Jersey's Mendham and Mt. Olive high schools.

DAVID LIEBMAN
A Life Unexpected

David Liebman started playing music—classical piano— at the age of 10. As a kid growing up in the Midwood section of Brooklyn, New York he took lessons at Bromley Studios of Music, about a mile away from home. "It was a family-run business, and I would go there on Saturdays," he recalls. Mrs. Bromley had connections enough to help David get gigs in "the mountains," which for a New Yorker meant only one thing: the Catskills. "For $15 a week, we played the summer when I was 13 years old. Saturday nights I would play Leonard's of Great Neck. That's where I learned the ropes." By the time he was 14, he owned a tux and was in the musicians' union. Initially, he was on his way to becoming a surgeon. "I had polio and spent a lot of time in hospitals. I had been exposed to doctors my whole life. The best thing you can be in a Jewish family is a doctor." But that all changed when he heard Coltrane play. "I wanted to know about jazz and get good at it. That's what changed my direction."

His self-described apprenticeship was also his biggest break, performing with Miles Davis, lasting a year and a half. This was on the tail end of being part of drummer Elvin Jones' group (Elvin played with John Coltrane's band). "Luck had a lot to do with it. I positioned myself for that. I lived in Manhattan, and I went to the right places," he says.

His tender age was not an issue because these masters were generous and kind. You were expected to work just as hard as everybody else, and you would eventually earn your stripes. "They'd check you out and see if you really mean it, by your attitude and the attention you paid to the music, and if you were prepared and took it seriously." You'll never meet anybody more open, warm, and sincere than jazz musicians, he adds.

David's muse has inspired him to achieve respectable authorship. His first venture was co-writing *Lookout Farm, A Case Study of Improvisation for Small Jazz Group* in the mid-1970s. His first offering as a solo writer, *Developing A Personal Saxophone Sound*

(Dorn Publications, 1989), was sparked by his experiences with "one of the greatest teachers of all time," a fellow by the name of Joe Allard who hailed from Lowell, Massachusetts. Joe was a clarinet and sax player who taught at Juilliard and the Manhattan School of Music. "He was a great guy. He taught a lot of famous cats. He was like a doctor. He told you what was wrong, and you fixed it." Later, David would write about the theory of chromatics and making sense of changing keys, captured in the 1991 *A Chromatic Approach to Jazz Harmony and Melody*. This book takes the principals of 20th-century jazz (composers like Béla Bartók) and helps the student explore what he or she can do in terms of Coltrane and other jazz artists. Chromatics offers a new realm of choices in harmony. "If I say, 'play a C7th chord,' I will give them a dozen ways to look at it logically and, hopefully, musically. It's taking what's there and making it appear a little differently—superimposing like a painter puts one thought over another, one color over another. It gives us much more of a palette when we are improvising."

How he got to Pennsylvania was a matter of two intersecting sets of circumstances. "I was 18 [in 1964] and my good piano player friend was working at [the former] Mt. Airy Lodge. He said 'we should come up.'" His buddy performed under Bob Newman, Mt Airy's band director at the time. "Bob was quite a jazz leader," recalls David. That was his intro to the Pocono Mountains.

His wife, oboist and English horn musician and composer Caris Visentin, also had connections to the area. She had visited the Poconos as a girl when she lived in nearby Palmerton Pennsylvania. She proposed the area as their new home, a place to get away from the city, yet be close enough to drive in for new gigs. The fact that there were jazz musicians here, when "anything west of the Hudson [River] is suspect," lent some credibility to the area. Besides, Caris knew the scene and that it was affordable "Stroudsburg is cool, she told me; you gotta know where to go. The dealmaker for taking the leap and moving was his first encounter with the Celebration of the Arts festival. With New York being pretty much a straight hour-plus across the highway, it was all eyes westward. Finding local work was not far behind. "My wife suggested that I do summer workshops here. I could go home for lunch." His classes at East Stroudsburg University attracted musicians from around the globe. On average, a select group of 1 participants are admitted. One requirement: they cannot be beginners. "They have to send me their composition so I can judge their level."

Finding work in the New York market is doable; one doesn't need to live in New York to play there, he reasoned. "This was a great move, and it became obvious I made the right decision. It's a life I didn't expect."

He's received two Grammy nominations, won the Jazz Journalists Award for Soprano Saxophone, and regularly hits many jazz publications' top awards time and again.

MT. AIRY LODGE
Igniting the Jazz Culture

If you lived in the New York metropolitan area in the 1970s, you may recall the now-quaint commercial describing the welcoming countryside getaway, "Beautiful Mt. Airy Lodge." With smiling people on ski lifts, it began: "Have a fine wintertime at the Poconos, at your host with the most in the Poconos." Constructed in 1898, in its heyday, Mt. Airy Lodge had an important role in the burgeoning Pocono jazz scene that began around the 1950s.

Bob Ferri worked as a facility manager and maintenance superintendent at Mt. Airy from 1977 until it closed in 2000. The honeymoon haven was widely known for playing host to the big bands and famed musicians. "People would say, oh my gosh he was here and she was here," recalled Ferri. The stream of big-time musicians went on and on: Pocono choral band master Fred Waring, Milton Berle, Tony Bennett, Bob Hope, Phyllis Diller, Rodney Dangerfield, Julio Iglesias. "If you name them, they were there." The nearby Paradise Stream Caesar's Resort booked major entertainment as well, but in terms of seating capacity, Mt. Airy Lodge had them all beat. One of its nightclubs could hold 1,000 people and the larger Crystal Room could accommodate 2,500. And for truly mammoth events, the Mt. Airy convention center could hold an impressive 8,000.

By comparison, "Paradise Stream could seat maybe 250," said Ferri. Appealing to mostly a family clientele, from the '70s to the '80s, Mt. Airy enjoyed an average guest stay of a week and sometimes longer. "In the '90s those weeks became three-day weekends," he noted. "The hotel tried hard to keep guests entertained there and provided them with every form of recreation so they would stay there rather than leave for other venues."

Susan Cooper, daughter of former co-owner Herman Martens, describes how the Martens family, whose previous generations came over from the Netherlands, took over the resort in the

1950s. She recalls it was a very cool place to grow up. "I basically worked in every department. We had to cross-train, so I went from accounting to waitressing to the front desk. I ended up being convention coordinator for weddings and banquets." From 1987 to 1996, a New York music promoter who booked entertainment on cruise ships, Bill Lockett, was responsible for securing the jazz talent at Mt. Airy. "He filled the entire place," says Susan. When Martens passed away in 1997, at a time when significant renovations were being made to the property, she took over and walked away when it was sold in 2000. Says Bill, former CEO of Travel and Entertainment Associates Inc. in Pine Hill, New Jersey, "It was a great place. I'm sorry it got caught up in the wayside of bad economic times."

"I stayed 'til the end," says Ferri. "It was sad to see the demolishing of a facility. I saw the business slide because people's demands have changed so much through the years. The facility did not change rapidly enough to stay ahead of the curve. We built hundreds of units in the '80s, when business was booming, all the honeymoon suites with heart-shaped tubs. We were building units and people were occupying it while the paint was still wet. It was quite a heady time. In the '90s, it started to take a slide to a point where they couldn't meet their financial obligations." Mt. Airy was then purchased by investors (Oaktree Capital of New York) who "tried to make a go of it," recalled Ferri. "They were unsuccessful, closed the doors in 2001 and put it up for sale for a number of years." Scranton businessman Louis DeNaples purchased the resort in 2004. Now the Mt. Airy Casino Resort sits on the footprint of the original hotel. Susan Cooper worked the pro shop there. While many big names headline at Mt. Airy today, the days of a well-worn migration pattern made by locally grown jazz musicians passing through to the Deer Head are gone.

Musings on the Creative Process

According to the encyclopedia of Jazz, improvisation has always been the life blood of jazz.

"Improv is 90% of what we do," says drummer Bill Goodwin. "But it doesn't drop out of the sky. You prepare. It comes out of your knowledge of the music and sensitivity to other musicians." At jam sessions at the Deer Head Inn, for example, Goodwin might call out a song his colleagues know. A key is quickly decided on, the tempo is counted, and off they go. "We improvise on the chord changes and make new melodies on that."

Sax talent Jay Rattman professes his love of improvising and speaks of two opposing philosophies that musicians often grapple with. "One is the ultimate goal to sound really polished and play perfectly even if it means it's not spontaneous, as long as it sounds good." At the other end of the spectrum is just being in the moment. "Be as creative as possible and run the risk of not sounding very good. But when you are *on,* it's an exciting thing." Jay values spontaneity over all else. "Most people wouldn't notice if it's not as polished. The best nights are when everybody's on and tuned in and it sounds like you've played this a million times before." The process involves finding one's own voice yet also being mindful of music history and theory. "Learn all the possibilities. But if you do that too carefully, it can be almost overwhelming. You can lose sight of what is genuine to you." Pure memorization is an academic exercise that's dry and hollow. "I continue to always sort it out, allowing myself to realize what is genuine and sincere and what is not, and getting rid of anything that's not."

Rick Chamberlain, who was a COTA co-founder and trombonist said the concept of improvisation didn't originate with jazz "Improv dates back to guys with powdered wigs getting together playing fugues in cutting sessions." Modern jazz gave improv a place to go: "Jazz is always going to evolve because people keep coming up with new ideas."

It's a conundrum. To develop one's own sound and style, the improvised material has to be recognizable as belonging to a particular musician. It doesn't have to be wildly different for each go 'round. Yet it's nearly impossible (and it's not desirable) to replicate a solo time and again. On developing a sound, Pocono-based tenor saxophone player Vinny Bianchi weighs in. Vinny had formed the Latin-groove band La Cuchina with keyboard player Marko Marcinko (an accomplished drummer), bass player Paul Rostock, Bill Washer on guitar, Dan Gonzales on drums, and Bob Velez on congas. Says Vinny, "I loved listening to Paul Desmond before I played the saxophone. My first sax was a tenor, so I started listening to Joe Henderson, Wayne Shorter and Sonny Rollins. You work to develop a centered sound that you are happy with, that's deep and rich."

Former COTA Cat and high school band director Lance Rauh discusses the creative process when had an epiphany at 30—literally, composing a symphony of that name. "When I was developing 'Epiphany' I had just turned 30 and was going through some life decisions. It was a very reflective summer." Lance was inspired by his advisor at Columbia University, Bert Konowitz (himself the composer of "Spirit"). Says Lance, "When I compose, I start with the melody and then write a bass line to fill it out. The saxes are heavy in epiphany and there is a trumpet solo." For the COTA Cats, he arranged three pieces. "I take the tune and apply my creative impression and interpretation of it." When he sought input from established Pocono composer Wolfgang Knittel (now passed; he wrote the choral operetta for the jazz mass which opened the Sunday festivities at the annual Celebration of the Arts) told Lance to go with his gut. "You'll figure it out," Lance recalls Wolfgang telling him. "If you like it, keep it. If not, change it."

There is some disagreement about whether "smooth jazz" is true jazz, but without argument, improv is involved in this genre too. Says smooth jazz drummer Tony Diecidue: "Improv is what I feel in the moment. If other players are really nailing it and the song is just grooving, it gives me the freedom to improvise and find more opportunity for creativity. But you can't let your musicians get lost since you are keeping the beat."

Phil Woods said the process of creating starts with the piano. He took the melody in his head and put it in a sketchpad along with countless other musical ideas. Then he used Sibelius 6 software to put it all together. However, one doesn't compose for jazz so much as *suggest themes* onto which the artist can improvise. He noted, "The first rule of jazz is to improvise. I was told to decorate the melodies of Benny Carter. Put your heart and soul in it."

JAY RATTMAN
From Russia with Love

It was very early on that Jay Rattman knew his first and most enduring love would be jazz.

At 10 days old, his parents took him to a Bob Dorough concert and when he was little, his grandmother Dorothy "Dotsie" Hauser took him to hear John Coates play piano at the Deer Head Inn. When sax master Phil Woods came out with his *Celebration* CD in 1998, 10-year-old Jay fell asleep to it, etching every nuance of each song onto his brain. "I knew the album inside and out. It's why I started sax." After, that is, taking clarinet, which in school was the prerequisite.

"Growing up around here, Phil Woods and Dave Liebman were personal influences for me. I grew up studying with them and have come to love the music of others like drummer Paul Motian and Lee Konitz (alto sax), Steve Lacy (soprano sax), Charlie Haden (double bass), Keith Jarrett . . . I could go on for hours."

Although neither of his parents were musicians, they are rabid jazz fans. On his mother's side is a line seven generations long of Russian Jewish string players, many of whom were classically trained at the Odessa Conservatory.

One of his forebears was Nathan "Tossy" Spivakovsky, a violin prodigy from the 1900s who, as a teen, developed a technique to bow double and triple stops, which changed the way musicians played Bach violin suites. He formed the Spivakovsky Duo along with his brother Jacob ("Jascha"), a pianist. A great uncle, Michael Spivakovsky, had a career in New York City as a violinist, performing as principal violin in some of Frank Sinatra's recordings and doing pit work on Broadway.

Now Jay plays soprano, alto, tenor, baritone and bass sax, as well as clarinet, bass clarinet and flute. He plays piano when he is studying a piece and when he is composing. He acknowledges the long, hard work in developing and perfecting the craft. An understanding of the back story is necessary as well. "In order to learn how to play you have to learn the history of the music and all sorts of different approaches. Learn all the possibilities. If you do that really carefully, it can be almost overwhelming; you can lose sight of what is genuine to you. I continue to sort it out, allowing myself to realize what is sincere and what is not, and getting rid of anything that's not."

Jay lives in New York City, a master's graduate of The Manhattan School of Music. Looking west, he says the Poconos is unique in being home to highly influential jazz figures. "You've got a handful of living legends who are recognized through the world as masters of their art, and they're just living in this otherwise normal area that's not an urban center. If you think about it, Phil Woods and Dave Liebman are NEA Jazz Masters. It's probably the highest per capita outside of New York City, even compared to Philly. Bob and Fay Lehr opened the Deer Head for jazz in 1955 and John Coates became their pianist. A scene sort of built around that."

Like his immensely talented ancestors, Jay makes his living through music. He plays in several jazz bands including his own quartet with piano, bass and drums, and a classical sax quartet. He also gives lessons and writes arrangements. "I wrote the string charts to go on a pop album that a friend of mine was working on. He sent me the tracks with the rhythm, singer, horns and guitar, and I wrote string parts to go on top of that." He transcribed a Keith Jarrett solo from "The Melody at Night with You" for a marimba player who wanted to perform it. If it's jazz he's working on, he consumes every recording he can find, either online, on a CD or on vinyl. On the classical side, his approach is to analyze and interpret it without any outside influences, later on perhaps researching other recordings of the piece. "There are a lot of unartful interpretations out there," he adds.

What's jazz, anyway? "Anything that wants to claim to be jazz, is jazz. A lot of people will disagree with that. I'm hesitant to say, because there are endless political battles in the jazz world about what is jazz and what is not. I don't exclude trends in European jazz or free jazz or fusion. I don't think it's fair to deny any of it." Smooth jazz? Yes, he admits, that too. "It happens to be crap, but it's still jazz. Jazz is not necessarily all good. It's a huge word."

Even now, in his successful career, he feels strongly about the singular reason for making music. "I love jazz and a lot of other music too. Ultimately you play music to do for other people what your favorite music has done for you, emotionally." Although he resides in New York, his collective family—both biological and musical—inhabits Pennsylvania. "I expect I'll always have a foot in the Poconos and play with musicians there."

NANCY REED
Music Among the Reeds (Part 1)

Vocalist and bass player Nancy Reed describes how she heard jazz and classical music every day, growing up in Brooklyn. "My mother liked opera. She sang a little and studied opera at the Chicago Conservatory. My father was a classical and jazz piano player, but not for a living." She found her first job in music singing at age 19. During her teens, she met guitarist and drummer Spencer Reed at a jam session in New York. They became friends, and when his career took him to the Poconos to play resorts, she followed. "He got a gig at Tamiment [Resort]. It was supposed to be a short gig, but one gig in the Poconos turned into 30 years."

In the years that "The Hustle" could be heard at every hotel and nightclub, Nancy found work on drums, but it wasn't what she really wanted to do. After several years on the Pocono circuit, the couple settled in, buying a home in Bushkill. By that time, Nancy learned the bass, and soon after she was introduced to the Pocono jazz community. "We were the first act at the first COTA, 40 years ago. Nobody got paid. It was just like playing in the street."

As to her inspiration, she notes, "Carmen McRae is my favorite. I also like Sarah Vaughan, Ella and Cleo Laine, and Mark Murphy taught me a lot about scatting."

Nancy and Spencer have played the Deer Head Inn as a duo, and she branched off into her own bands like the Bobettes and 3spirit, which started as the backup band for pianist Bob Dorough. She also sings with the Duke Ellington Legacy band (with Duke's grandson), has played Mexico's Cancun Jazz Festival, has toured Italy with pianist Dave Leonhardt, and she gives voice lessons. She and Spencer composed a tune that appeared on her CD *Blue Sunrise*, and they appear on Bob Dorough's *Schoolhouse Rock Earth*. Nancy has collaborated with NEA Jazz Master David Liebman on the CD *Neighbors*, and she says, "He's fabulous to work with."

"It was always music. I never wanted to do anything else. I'm so fortunate I almost can't believe I get to do this."

SPENCER REED
Music Among the Reeds (Part 2)

Spencer Reed plays a steady beat with his guitar, emphasizing low F in the "Sunshine of Your Love" opening strains. "Catch that scoopy thing," he says as one note slides up a half-step. He's talking to a roomful of student musicians dubbed "The Blue Note" group at Camp Jazz. To the drummer of the group, he adds, "Maybe keep the high hat going, ride real light in the cymbal. We don't really need that F. Instead, bump it down and leave out the top voice."

A respected jazz and blues musician, it was not the first summer that Spencer mentored high school students during the one-week summer program at Camp Jazz. He has a lot to say about his own education. "School was horrible, and I didn't want to go. But when they taught me how to read music, it made sense," he recalls. "In grade school, we learned on a little plastic tonette, which I still have." His musical life began at age six when he heard Charlie Parker, Dave Brubeck and Coleman Hawkins. At 12, he learned guitar because his brother played it. Yet at first, he thought his future was in medicine. "Until age 15, I was sure I was going to be a doctor. But in my first years of high school, I realized wanted to be a musician."

Born in the Bronx, New York, he was playing professionally at age 18 when he freelanced first as a singer (and later, on the guitar) for the soul Distributors. Spencer smiles as he remembers his key part in those days on "Me and Mrs. Jones": the harmony line a "(we've got a) thing going on." Then he played with the Chris Towns Unlimited band with superstars Jimmy Lewis (who worked with Count Basie) and Kalil Madi (former drummer for Billie Holiday). In 1976, he was "dragged" to the Poconos, this time as a drummer. "I met an agent, a good friend of mine, who introduced me to agent Stanley Flato at the union floor of the Roseland Ballroom. He was the partner of Hy Einhorn, who handled all big acts. They were like cousins. He said, 'too bad you're not a drummer, I have a full-time job for you.'" Not one t pass up such an opportunity, Spencer says, "That's when I moved to Tamiment on a day's notice. It was extreme culture shock. I had hardly heard of the Poconos." Tamiment represents an important piece of the musical history of the region. "Sid Caesar, Imogene Coca, Dick Shawn and Norman Lear wrote weekly plays at the Tamiment with the originators of the TV shows from the 1940s. That started the migration from the New York area." Spencer worked six nights a week at Tamiment. "It was a small band at Tamiment, the David Charles Trio [a New York band]. I also played with Bob Boucher who had been the band leader at New York's Roxy Theatre. We played big band material." In those early days, Spencer and wife Nancy lived on-site at Tamiment. Nancy is a renowned jazz vocalist and bassist, the other half of their self-named performing duo. When they first formed Nancy and Spencer Reed, they both played guitar and sang. "The only publicity I had, was going up and down Route 611 and Route 209 and stopping everywhere that there was a bar. Steve Jakubowitz gave me work at the Tannersville Inn. It became the place to play jazz." When Steve heard Nancy sing, he said, "What's that scat thing you're doing? Do it more."

Another stroke of opportunity brought Spencer to the Delaware Water Gap jazz scene. This occurred when he was approached by the late Ed Joubert, a co-founder of the Celebration of the Arts and owner of the bar/restaurant The Bottom of the Fox, where Nancy and Spencer were the Friday night band. "It was Ed who asked Nancy and me to play at the first COTA festival. This was pivotal for us. It was our first direct association with the legends who lived up the road," a reference to Phil Woods and Rick Chamberlain, both passed. Other local work included jobs he got from singer Jerry Harris, who helped jump-start the gigs with his enthusiasm. Later on, he reached a cherished goal by making it to the Deer Head Inn with the help of Chris and Donna Solliday when they owned it; Spencer and Nancy played there on Sundays for three years. He also played the weekly blues jam at the Deer Head for five years running, and it's also where he developed his signature throaty vocal style. "I can't say enough about the Deer Head. It's been an honor to play there."

Combining a love of music with his skill for teaching, Spencer served as director of the band programs at the Notre Dame and

Monsignor McHugh High Schools in East Stroudsburg. Top on his list of classroom priorities was teaching students a sense of discipline. "Some are shocked that you have to practice. I love watching their eyes light up when they get it right."

Spencer is inspired by greats Charlie Parker and Django Reinhardt and his own brother who guided him when he first picked up the guitar, in addition to the "three gems" who years ago made the Poconos their home: Phil Woods, David Liebman and Bob Dorough of *Schoolhouse Rock!* renown. In 2009, Dorough recorded a new version of the popular cartoon series, and Spencer played a few tracks, providing the vocals for a rapping grizzly bear.

In 2009, he collaborated with baritone sax player Roger Rosenberg (who performed with steely Dan) on the blues CD *People Just Don't Like Me*. Says Spencer, "I was going to do a solo album. Roger and I had lunch at Camp Jazz. He asked me, 'Where are you going to record the album?'" One thing led to another and now Roger played all but one track on the blues-based compilation, released in the spring of 2011.

"I've always felt it is a privilege that I make a living playing music," Spencer adds.

The View Across the Oceans: An International Footnote

Lena Bloch is a sax sensation from Europe who is now living in Brooklyn. Her connection to the Poconos was an indirect one: a 1991 workshop given by NEA Jazz Master David Liebman in Holland. "He was teaching his sound production ideas which were put together in his book *Developing a Personal Saxophone Sound*. It is as useful as it is beautiful and inspiring," says Lena. "Dave is an unforgettable artist, once you meet him. Very powerful, sincere and inspiring."

Having left Russia over 40 years ago, Lena dons her signature tuxedo and plays clubs throughout New York City, meeting up with her many musician friends who relocated from places like Belgium, Israel, Holland, Germany, Italy and Canada. "I liked the way music is felt in the US. There is a strong feeling that music has a purpose different than entertainment, that the audience is as much involved in the process as musicians themselves are. People outside the US were tremendously attracted to that feeling of participation and involvement."

The appeal of American jazz is intense the world over, opines Zhi Yong Zhang, a 50-year-old musician and teacher from Hong Kong. He was fortunate to receive a scholarship to study at Boston's Berklee College of Music (in fact, in 2000, he was the first student from China to have graduated from Berklee). Zhi plays flute, the Chinese bamboo and pan flutes, clarinet and sax. He taught at Hong Kong International Christian Quality secondary and Primary Music school, and the Hong Kong Institute of education; served as assistant professor at Xinghai Conservatory of Music in Guangzhou, China; and is a composer and recording artist. His view of jazz is expressed in the following quote:

"I think jazz is a great treasure that the American people dedicated to the whole world. I consider famous musicians like Miles Davis, John Coltrane and Charlie Parker to be very important names, and every musician should know them as they know Bach and Mozart. In so many countries, jazz music has already become a major subject in school, but in Hong Kong, I'm still looking forward to it. I wish I could teach students what I learned at Berklee. I want to become a real 'jazz messenger.'"

FRED WARING
Enunciate, Communicate, Sing

Imagine being a little kid who is lucky enough to be part of a musically historical moment in time, one that defined the American choral sound of the '30s and '40s. Malcolm Waring had many memorable years doing just that as he tagged along with his dad, band leader Fred Waring, and his wall of sound act known as Fred Waring and the Pennsylvanians. "It was all around me," Malcolm recalls. "One of the biggest treats was to go on the road with him two or three weeks every year. When they went on tour, I'd hop on the bus when they came through Palm Springs, travel with them through southern and northern California, then fly back. I'd take my schoolwork with me, but I never did much of it." The band members, comprised of the singers and orchestra musicians, took him under their wing. "There were a lot of one-night gigs and bus riding. I got a pretty good appreciation of how much work is involved." During performances, Malcolm wandered backstage, sometimes hanging out with lighting and sound guys, sometimes helping to sell programs.

Fred wrote some original compositions and also performed some covers, with a lot of standards (Cole Porter, Rodgers and Hart), often closing out a show with a choral version of "The Battle Hymn of the Republic." The many women in the chorus—among them, one Miss America—were outfitted by his wife. Virginia Waring was not a seamstress by trade, though. She was a concert pianist and Fred's stand-in conductor. (Notably, when Fred passed away, after several writers attempted to memorialize his lifetime of achievements, she became the author of the 2007 *Fred Waring and the Pennsylvanians, Music in American Life* published by the University of Illinois Press.) The Pennsylvanians had a definable style of blending voices known as the Waring Sound. "It's about using tone syllables, a specific technique," says Malcolm. "It came about because he felt you should be able to understand all the words in a song."

The band leader enjoyed giving his summer workshops, ensuring a steady stream of available talent. According to the 1983 program "Fred Waring, A Musical Pioneer," his educator program helped young singers develop their sound to his glee club standards. It read: "Workshoppers learn each day what might take the average school chorus a month to learn. In 12 days, young singers learn and absorb the involved elements of a professional level production. On the final two evenings, they stage a skilled performance far beyond the expectations of the audience and critics." Adults were able to take classes on the finer points of choral techniques, and a five-day session instructed on movement and choreography. The Ennis David staff scholarships were awarded to 10 musicians comprising the Workshop Blendors [spelling intentional] who spent the summer on the main campus of Penn State and became "polished pros."

Fred Waring didn't just invent the famous choral sound that found its way from radio and TV to concert halls and theaters and on albums with labels like Victor, Decca, Capital and Reprise. He founded Shawnee Press, which became a major music publisher. It was sold in 1989 and ultimately became absorbed by the Hal Leonard Corporation. He is also widely known for perfecting and marketing a blender called the Waring Blendor. Fred developed the product by creating its distinctive cloverleaf jar and seal. The blender's uses were not confined to the kitchen, as it occupied a role in developing serums to treat Yellow Fever and Rocky Mountain Spotted Fever. Another original: the concept of the popular concert tour, which Malcolm states his dad started in 1948. According to the 1983 program, it was a different way of reaching Americans. It took the stuffiness out of the word *concert* and blazed the way for other artists.

There's more. Fred employed his architectural talents to convert an old carriage house to a charming country retreat called The Gatehouse. He and his wife and children spent four months there each year; otherwise, the family resided in Palm Springs. He was also an avid golfer and was said to have hit 12 holes in one. And, a devotee of comic strips, Fred invited the National Cartoonists Society to Shawnee. For over 30 years, the organization met there annually around his birthday.

"He just loved to entertain people," says Malcolm. "When he finally figured it was time to retire, he had a farewell tour . . . then the next year said he wasn't ready and went out on the road again." He had a lot of music in him to the very end.

PHIL WOODS
In the Gap, the Man with the Hat

He played a Yamaha 82z alto sax which he said was incredible, and used #3 Vandoren reeds. Named NEA Jazz Master in 2007, Phil Woods (who has almost too many career highlights to capture) also received the Mellon Jazz Living Legacy Award. Toward the end of a successful career, he reflected on a long and interesting career, and stated he learned a valuable lesson from dear friend Benny Carter. "Benny was a great alto player. I once asked him why did you do it? He said, to be a cultured human being."

Phil was a grad of Juilliard and moved to New Hope, PA, in the 1950s. From 1961 to 1966, he ran the jazz program at the arts camp at Ramblerny (formerly the Maynard Ferguson School of Jazz), in Bucks County, Pennsylvania. It was there he met 14-year-old Rick Chamberlain (co-founder of Delaware Water Gap's Celebration of the Arts). "It was across from Frenchtown [New Jersey] on a lovely old estate with swimming pools. It was wonderful." Many graduates became well-known in the music world. "When they closed it in 1967, it kind of broke my heart. My son would have had free tuition and I could get off the road. This reinforced my decision to move to Europe in 1968." So it was off to Paris, to get away from the violence of the 1960s. Why France? During World War II, he explains, the very talented infantry band that the United States sent to France marked the first time the French heard jazz. "Then on the Voice of America with Willis Conover, they would broadcast jazz all over the world. The benefit of war is that it spreads our music all over the planet. We educated the world about jazz and the lesson is freedom with responsibility."

He returned to the States in 1972; first stop, California. "I had a disastrous time in Los Angeles. For some reason, I wanted a house with a pool." He was almost headed back to France when composer and pianist Michel Legrand offered him a gig in the Poconos. Phil had met future wife Jill Goodwin in California and with the work back East, they moved to the Poconos in October 1973. "I always had a tie to Pennsylvania through the Deer Head

Inn, where I played when I was living in New Hope. Jerry Vale would need an extra sax, and they'd bring a couple of us guys from New Hope. We did Mt. Airy, then went afterwards to play at the Deer Head."

The man's fingers sure could fly up and down the horn. To get to that stage, he said, it was diligent practicing, done slowly. "Tell each finger where to move and be patient. And memorize the music." Aretha Franklin, Billy Joel and Steely Dan all shared space on his iPod, but the genre known as smooth jazz did not impress. "It's more market shit. It's not music, not jazz and not smooth. That's not to say there might not be some very good sax players, but basically, it's showbiz."

Phil—known by the moniker "The Man With The Hat"—stopped teaching privately as he aged. "I play as well as I can, talk it up and give lectures." Not one to hide his opinions, the Man with the Hat offered this advice to young and hopeful musicians. "Before you dash off to college, you might consider getting on a steamer with whatever it is you play and learn to play for your supper. Be able to paint a little bit, speak a foreign language, try to understand women . . . that last one is impossible, but I try. You're not just a sax. You must be able to put into your music something that's going on in your life."

He admitted doing a lot of preaching. "I think it's most important that I speak with my sax. You have to have the fire in the belly at an early age. But even for a middle-aged person who likes to play sax, it's all in line with being a cultured human being and taking part in the experience of making music with other people."

"Music is never going to go away. We need it like we need fresh air and water. Jazz is the only thing that is uncontaminated. It's not for sale."

Phil Woods passed away in 2015.

Postscript
A Musical History of the Author

Typically, the story of how a book came about resides before the text itself. However, the more I delved into the jazz heritage of one little corner of Pennsylvania, the more fascinating it was, even beyond my first hunches. And so I thought that tracing jazz's roots in the Poconos deserved its place front and center without my personal musings delaying the tale. But now, to wrap up, here goes.

I was totally inspired to write *The Poconos in B Flat* because of my genetic interest in the arts which I owe to my dad. Save for prattling into a bugle during his service in the Merchant Marines, he exhibited no real musical inclinations. Yet, he was the most creative person I knew growing up. Irving was a published freelance writer for the fashion trades and mystery magazines, an amateur photographer and a talented artist who worked in pastels and oils, causing the smell of turpentine to perpetually waft throughout our ample five-room apartment in Brooklyn. He believed good New York parents dragged their kids to the Metropolitan Museum of Art, the Guggenheim and the Jewish Museum. His eyes lit up whether he offered an interpretation of a painting or commented on a suit of armor, and he indulged my fascination with unicorn tapestries and told me about pointillism and op art. For a finale, he published his only novel months before he died. He is my hero.

I was nurtured on classical music. Unspellable, consonant-clashing names tumbled out of my dad's mouth and onto our stodgy turntable, providing samples of Dvorak, Mussorgsky, Tchaikovsky and others. These albums were leaden vinyl plates where low notes were known to snare the needle to a complete stop. My brain soaked up the tunes that my father whistled through his teeth. From time to time, I find myself humming them without realizing even where they came from.

My dad succumbed to pancreatic cancer when I was 14. He was a young 47 just hitting his artistic stride. I'm blessed to have a very special musical memory of his last struggling days. My mom asked me to play violin for him in an old-fashioned salon setting, so I set to practicing a few tunes on my school-quality fiddle (cheap rental that it was). I scratched out a meager attempt at music to a living room full of relatives. The kicker was that, unfortunately, I was not told this was my swan song, as he was near the end of his days. Had I understood the finality of my performance I surely would have been far too devastated to perform, to say nothing of the inherent pressure in such a situation. I played "The Ash Grove," badly, squeakily, forgettably. I played Bach's "Arioso," which has remained one of my favorites. When I play it on the sax now, correcting for a prior lack of expressiveness, my eyes well up with tears.

In my early school career, I cut my teeth on a few instruments. Who can forget the '60s academic favorite, the tonette? (See Spencer Reed's chapter above.) Then in second grade, when asked what I'd like to try among the percussion family, I chose the symbols, to be proudly smashed together during the high points of John Philip Sousa's "The Thunderer." It only required a modicum of dexterity, a keen watch on the conductor and a willingness to risk embarrassment should the cue be missed. I remember the rush that shot through me at the concert when my part approached. Afterward, I knew I wanted to replicate that glorious thrill as often as possible. This is the start of something, I told myself.

In fourth grade it was the clarinet. The keys seemed to be arranged in a disorganized and unintuitive manner, at least to a novice. Huff and harf as I might, for weeks I could not get anything resembling a note out of it. In fifth grade, I took a safer route, opting for chorus.

Saying goodbye to elementary school and moving on up to junior high was an exciting time. The B44 Nostrand Avenue bus whisked me off to Kings Highway to the big kids' annex for seventh graders. It was here that I started violin. We huddled in the music classroom, directly off the boiler room in the basement. The teacher seemed to be a humorless loner who never doled out praise and seemed physically unable to crack a smile (later, I learned this wasn't true, so heartfelt apologies to Mr. K.). I was convinced he auditioned the class often just to terrify us, eliciting regular attacks of dread among the students. When it was my turn, the chin rest became so slippery from sweat that I thought the whole fiddle would slide out from under my grip and fling itself into the person to my left, blinding the poor sap. Yet somehow, I got out of junior high alive (musically speaking). I counted myself lucky that my teacher's apparent lack of pleasure in his career choice did not turn me off from music.

I continued violin in high school. The instrument was so popular among my classmates that we ended up with two nice-sized violin sections. I was in the second violin group and quickly rose to section leader (auditions had now lost the intimidation factor). The seconds were responsible for harmonizing with the musical lead of the first violins, and for the first time I really felt the excitement of playing "in an orchestra."

In my mid-20s, I found myself divorced, seeking a productive distraction. I scrabbled together enough of my municipal pay (I was a probation officer with a tepid salary) and headed to Manny's on 47th Street in Manhattan to purchase an alto sax. I chose the alto because I thought it was cool; the tenor is too big, the soprano too shrill. Clarinets reminded me of my early shriek-like results. The flute, well, there are an obnoxious number of ledger lines that sit atop the staff, and I am not up to the task of counting them all.

The saxes gleamed from Manny's second-story windows, catching the afternoon sunlight that spilled between the buildings on the West Side of the city. The angels sighed, drawing me body and soul into this place that countless musicians—hopefuls, wannabes and success stories—came and went. It felt exactly that poetic to me.

I decided to look for instruction as near as possible to the landmark that said *jazz* to me, the Washington Square archway under which musicians can be heard playing almost any instrument any day of the year. The Mannes College's New School for Social Research offered pay-as-you-go sax lessons. I could get there from the probation office in a few bus stops. Though it was the wrong direction as far as heading home, there was nothing rushing me back to Brooklyn.

The New School was a small building crunched between

buildings comprising the NYU campus, which spread over several city blocks. The teacher was this guy Ken who claimed to be in the Stone Poneys band before Linda Ronstadt made it big. We'd pass the sax back and forth (switching mouthpieces) as I learned the basics: first, the scale of C since it had no accidentals, then adding the keys that use F sharp, C sharp, B flat (my favorite "blue note"), the octave key. I already knew how to read music but coaxing a sound out of the instrument was a challenge; I'd not be deterred by having fallen short on the clarinet. Prematurely, I felt, Ken brought out a sheet of paper that read "Desafinado." What I thought was a commentary on how most people play it ("Slightly Out of Tune") or maybe a scribbled note not meant for me to see was actually its English translation. Ken patiently watched me struggle like hell through the piece, damn those accidentals. Don't even ask me about "Ornithology," which he smoothly and speedily showcased for me. Initially a distraction from my new single status, the affection I was developing for my sax provided fulfillment that invaded me on the cellular level.

Coming up with a month's rent every two pay cycles moved front and center as I was now residing divorced and alone in the downstairs "newlywed" apartment of a two-story brick home owned by a terminally cranky old couple. Inconveniently, my $400 rent left little wiggle room for the weekly $25 forays at the New School and so after a brief period of musical sunshine lasting three months, I said goodbye to Ken and snapped my case shut, putting the horn away for what would be decades.

When I picked it up again more than 20 years later, it was like being reunited with an old friend. The Conn had been good to me and held some lovely recollections. But as I progressed, I grew tired of its tinny quality. This time I took myself to a music store in Nazareth, Pennsylvania and tried out the top-of-the-line horns. The most excruciatingly expensive horn turned out not to be my favorite. With several paychecks stashed away and a generous contribution from my fan base (Mom), I chose a Yamaha.

How long before one is promoted out of the amateur classification: is it the number of paid gigs you've snagged or is it a function of time? Is the tipping point when you can master some monstrously fast Charlie Parker? My level still firmly resides in the happy amateur category. But I'm not worried. The Yamaha fits me like a glove, and the sound is pure velvet.

I loved jazz so much that I decided to write my first book— this book—about it; a jazzy love letter to the Poconos. At the time of this second edition, I have written a total of nine books, mostly about jazz, in both fiction (three novels) and three nonfiction books. Of the latter, the series *Tasty Jazz Jams for Our Times* will see a new volume (Vol. 3) by the end of 2023. In 2016, I started my jazz blog, which has hundreds of personal interviews with musicians around the world, including iconic household names (Sonny Rollins, Houston Person, Ron Carter, Jane Ira Bloom, Christian McBride, Betty Bryant, and more) as well as emerging artists and everyone in between. They come from countries like Israel, Greece, South Africa, Norway, France, etc. and they play all types of instruments and all subgenres. Find the blog at debbieburkeauthor.com.

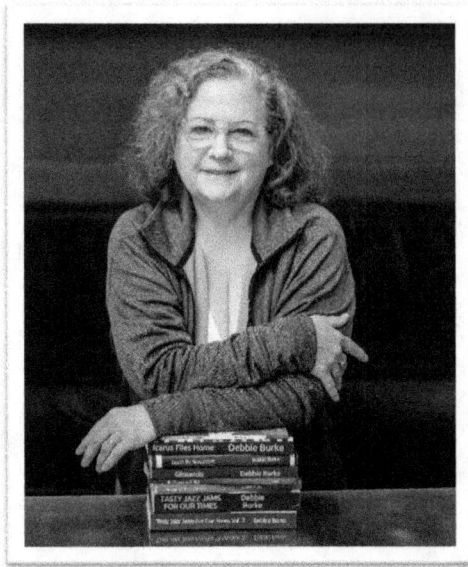

ABOUT THE AUTHOR

Debbie Burke is a Brooklyn-born writer who lived for over 20 years in the Pocono Mountains of Pennsylvania. While there, she wrote a column about her musical experiences called "Midlife Sax," co-founded Artsmash of the Poconos, created the Pocono Jazz and Poetry website, and played in three community bands until the university killed the music program. Debbie has written hundreds of columns and articles and was the editor of an award-winning business journal. This was her first book. Today, she is an award-winning author of nine books, mostly about jazz, in fiction and nonfiction, and a professional editor at Queen Esther Publishing LLC. She occasionally picks up that Yamaha.

ABOUT THE COVER ARTIST

Born and raised in Brooklyn, NY, **Ka-son Reeves** grew up cultivating his natural artistic ability by watching the creative processes of his father, a portrait artist, and his eldest brother, a local graffiti artist. They served as Ka-son's artistic teachers and technical advisors. Ka-son has participated in dozens of solo and group exhibitions and won numerous painting awards. His art (www.artofkason.com) has been featured in many galleries throughout the Poconos, New York, New Jersey and others. He now expresses himself as a painter using the acrylic medium. He painted "Maxine" in 2010, which is featured on the front cover.

Ka-son's statement: "My art represents the myriad spirit and emotion of urban life, with an emphasis on life, as seen through my eyes, imagined in my mind and felt in my heart. That life in my art is not limited to any one physical location, but expanded upon in an attempt to embrace a universal perspective."

ABOUT MAXINE SULLIVAN

Swing singer Maxine Sullivan was born in Homestead, Pennsylvania in 1911 and died in New York City in 1987. She is best known for taking the Scottish folk tune "Loch Lomond" and making it her own with her smooth singing style and elegant phrasing. It is not known if she ever performed in the Pocono region but the decision to have her on the cover is a wish that perhaps, in traveling across the state to perform in New York City in the 1980s, she did grace the clubs here with her presence. Besides, the author has a small but harmless obsession with Ms. Sullivan and her music.